POETRY now

IMAGES IN MOTION

Edited by

Heather Killingray

First published in Great Britain in 2000 by
POETRY NOW
Remus House,
Coltsfoot Drive,
Woodston,
Peterborough, PE2 9JX
Telephone (01733) 898101
Fax (01733) 313524

All Rights Reserved

Copyright Contributors 2000

HB ISBN 0 75430 975 4
SB ISBN 0 75430 976 2

FOREWORD

Although we are a nation of poets we are accused of not reading poetry, or buying poetry books. After many years of listening to the incessant gripes of poetry publishers, I can only assume that the books they publish, in general, are books that most people do not want to read.
Poetry should not be obscure, introverted, and as cryptic as a crossword puzzle: it is the poet's duty to reach out and embrace the world.
The world owes the poet nothing and we should not be expected to dig and delve into a rambling discourse searching for some inner meaning.
The reason we write poetry (and almost all of us do) is because we want to communicate: an ideal; an idea; or a specific feeling. Poetry is as essential in communication, as a letter; a radio; a telephone, and the main criterion for selecting the poems in this anthology is very simple: they communicate.

CONTENTS

A Mermaid's Tale	Caryne Crane	1
Old Friend	Joe De La Mare	2
A Blessing Indeed	Josephine Foreman	3
Portrait Of A Friend	Debbie Perks	4
Untied Navel Strings	Ken Draffin	5
At The Eiffel Tower	Carole Luke	6
Bitter-Sweet Refrain	Maroushka Monro	7
Just A Housewife	Cindy White	8
One Death Too Many	Dee Yates	9
The Picturesque	Jean P McGovern	10
Magic	Janis Smith	11
Our Pets	C C Lee	12
Happy Families	Karen Hunton	13
Perseverance	Hywel Davies	14
Circles Of Life	Margaret Jackson	15
Zodiac Reflections: . . .	Jackie J Docherty	16
A Dog's Life	Ian Stewart	18
War Games	Brenda Dove	19
Painting	Betty Green	20
Woolly Bite	Ivy Lott	21
The Isle Of Shells	Rianne Cannon	22
Jacko's Holiday	Kathleen M Hatton	23
Cook-In-Charge	Kathy Twist	24
In Harmony	Margaret Cowan	25
Dunkirk: A Child's Eye View	Pam Redmond	26
Disturbance	Margaret Gurney	27
True Story: In A Flap!	K Pusey	28
Sand Of Red	A May	29
First Meeting	S Mullinger	30
Butterflies	Sophie Cara Nicolaysen	31
The Story Of Silver	Lisa-Marie Corcoran	32
My Beautiful Day	Audrey Bowden	33
Banter At Her Majesty's . . .	Alfa	34
Ming's Evening Out	Jean Wearn Wallace	35
The Harp	Carole Revell	36
Hide And Seek!	Glan Grey Jones	37

Our True Love	Brian Marshall	38
Marrakech Movies	Margaret Whitaker	39
Grand Prix	Ron Bissett	40
The Gladeye	Colin Skilton	41
And Finally Empathy	Vie Tulloch	42
Interview	S M Thompson	43
The Bombs	W I Cooksey	44
She Hides Her Children	Marcus Tyler	45
The Pool	Gwyneth Box	46
The Ferryman	Susan Kemp	47
A Priceless Friendship	Brenda Robson-Eifler	48
Endless Deserts	Thomas Harrison	49
The Happening	Jenni A Rose	50
If Only	Janet Hewitt	52
Wasted Years	Alan Palmer	53
Parents	Winifred Tutte	54
The Day I Saw The Eclipse . . .	Patricia Jones	55
Surprises	Mary Marriott	56
We Bought A House	Elizabeth Hudson	57
Stolen Cherries	Leslie Fine	58
Lambo	Duncan C Callander	60
My Mate Charlie	Julia Pattison	61
Dragon From Hell	Kendric Ross	62
A Child Of The Thirties	Pat Heppel	63
The Park	A Cotter	64
Three Wishes	Tricia	65
Mrs Noah's Jumble Sale	Joyce Walker	66
A Consequential Tale	Jim Sargant	67
Carmody's Vision	Jacquie Williams	68
Ode To HRT	Maureen Davis	69
Out Of The Blue	Jackie Warren	70
Maisey	Jane Birch	71
The Return	Channon Cornwallis	72
Bengie Tabby Cat's Close Shave	Linda Brown	74
My Grandfather	Pamela M Henderson	75
Just Passing By	W M Francis	76
To My Darling Husband . . .	Heather Feetham	78
The Owl	Twaa Bowcock	79

My Mum	Jill K Gilbert	80
Hated Simply For Being Me	Jane Smith	82
Kanada	Kenny Morrison	83
Grandma	Gill Morgan	84
Precious Moment	Patricia Whittle	85
Wartime Oasis	Dora Hawkins	86
My Aunt And Uncle's House	Paul Wilkins	87
Happy Birthday Mum	Lin Bisgrove	88
Say Thank You . . .	Ghazanfer Eqbal	89
The Heirloom	Karin-Anne McFadden	90
Disquieted Rest	Louise Rogers	91
Our Lilley	R A Toy	92
Millie	S A Doughty	93
Thank You For Being My . . .	Barbara Huntley	94
Untitled	Bessie Thackeray	95
Veronica's Poem	Peter Steele	96
Family Roots	Terry Daley	97
Elements Of Identity	Naomi Elisa Price	98
Crossed Wires	Jean Paisley	99
Tea With Alexander (Aged Six)	Mary Hughes	100
My Dearest Love	Janet Robertson Jones	101
Vicky, Ben And I	Ian K A Ferguson	102
My Peaceful Memories	Irene Low	103
Free Indeed	Jeremy Jones	104
Back The Strand	Brandan O'Neill	106
Its Power	Kulsum Shaikh	107
Reverie	Breanach	108
A Nightingale Kept In A Cage	Rodger Moir	109
Growing Old	E Budd	110
Unknown Wealth	David Hazlett	111
The Unemployed	Janet Elaine Hill	112
My Great Grandma	Lauren Beevers	113
Who Are You?	A Buttress	114
Ode To Ego	Hazel Tealby	115
Imagination	Jacqueline Jeffs	116
Sunlight	Sheila Cheetham	117
Dusty	Rod Trott	118
A Magic Wand	A McMaster	119

The Minus And The Plus	Joan Harland	120
I'm Going To Become A Poet . . .	Rizwana Yunis	121
School Hols Again!	Janet Daniels	122
Victoria Falls	Alex Branthwaite	123
But A Dream	Angus Crawford	124
The Dome	Shauneen Maria Mitchell	125
Princess	Jack Purdom	126
The Library	Joy M Jordan	127
Betrayal	Veronica Daniel	128
For Her Money	Joan Wylde	129
Birdsong	Diana Price	130
Electrical Heaven	Lesley-Ann Curdy	131
Renewal At Nine O'Clock	Judy Studd	132
One . . .	Ria Blackwell	133
School Yard	Damian Begley	134
The Enchanting Spring	Edna O'Hara	135
The Rose	GIG	136
Will To Win	Peter J Sutton	137
Paean To The Generations	Seán Rooney	138
Dementia	A J French	139
Poetic Posers	John P Evans	140
Goodbye	Jessica Graham	141
Gossip Is Life	T Burke	142
A Life	Sheila Burnett	143
Doubting Thomas	Winifred Lund	144
Dalek Country	Ali Sebastian	146
Age Of Destruction	Karen Brooke	147
Impromptu Departure	Sheila Spence	148
Dead Man Coughing	Thomas Wyche	149
My Burning Love	Anne McTavish	150
Please Don't Go	Ken Mills	151
The Bodyguard	Frank Jensen	152
Top Of The Stairs	B G Clarke	153
Morning Mists	Carol Olson	154
Waiting	Muriel Turner	155
A Nice Wee Cat	Eleanor Dunn	156
Remember Her	Betty Worley	157
Cat Capone	Marageret Phillips	158

Reflection	Robert D Shooter	159
Loneliness!	M Muirhead	160
After Life	Darren Abbott	161
Intertravelling	Miriam Thornicroft	162
The Authentic Western Night	Don Goodwin	163
Newcastle Staffs Carnival	Marie Barker	164
Frogger!	Christine Wayne	165
Supernatural	Amy Holland	166
Who Needs Reflexology	Paff	167
The Slab	Gloria Hargreaves	168
The Closing Summer Day	Joanne Collinson	170

A Mermaid's Tale

As the sea lashes with passion against the rocks
Silently she appears, resting her weary, lifeless tale
Her skin like marble, hair of golden silky locks
A sparkle like crystal from every scale
As her beauty shines so much misery can be seen
Her swelling eyes so full of tears
Instead of accepting what should have been
They chose to banish her for a hundred years
Her only crime, a man from the land above
Their lives are only ever shared at night
His eyes caught hers and from then was love
When he leaves, her loneliness returns by morning light
A decision she's made, life without him she cannot bear
Her choice to end it all as her dreams she cannot fulfil
But still there is no choice, either above or below, they cannot share
Life above with him would be more painful still
With her eyes closed, her mind a blur, she quietly starts to pray
Pain and hurt eating at her, tearing her anxiously in two
Her body dissolves within the tide, her thoughts now a world away
A life planned for the future she never could go through
Her lover now returns to an empty shore, his life he chooses to take
Seeing as she lies as a bed of roses, the rocks she gently paves
At last in death together, walking on velvet sands at daybreak
Look closely to the ocean depths, see their beauty amongst the waves
Two souls now reunited in a world where they belong
Together now for eternity, their paths will no longer drift
No denying an everlasting love, for their world's too strong
Calm waters and the reddest sunsets for us their gift.

Caryne Crane

OLD FRIEND

Faithful old friend, faithful and true,
The time as come to part, to say adieu.
For twenty years you've pulled my cart,
But now the time has come for us to part.
We've been together these many long years,
We've shared our troubles, our joys, our fears.
Between the shafts you steadily trot,
You've not asked for much or for a lot,
Just a place to rest your weary head,
A heap of straw on which to make your bed.
A drink of water from the trough,
And then once more we will be off.
Life for you was once complete
When you had a bale of hay to eat.
You never complained whatever the load,
You never complained however long the road,
It did not matter how steep the hill,
You pulled and pulled and pulled until,
Until at last we reached the top,
And when 'Whoa' I cried, you would then stop.
Through wind and rain and sun and snow,
Onwards, onwards, ever onwards you did go.
You are the best friend I ever had,
it is because of this that I am sad.
All the good times now are past,
The time to part has come at last,
For as the years they unfold,
I fear we are both getting old.
Old friend, you have done your very best,
But now the time has come for you to rest.
The time has come to say adieu,
Faithful old friend, faithful and true.

Joe De La Mare

A Blessing Indeed

Everything is falling into place
Giving one a new face
Life has turned
To the kind I yearned
'Tis a wonderful feeling
Sends one reeling

Keeping in line
I had for some time
Felt that a change would be
As I now see
A blessing indeed
Which I did need

Following nature
I see a new future
And without being coy
I am filled with joy
I studied my position well
And everything seems swell

New friends I have found
No time to frown
As I continue my journey
Through life whatever may be
I see the sunshine
And feel sublime.

Josephine Foreman

PORTRAIT OF A FRIEND

Falling into yourself, eager to please
The guests. Running around serving
Drinks, food and changing the record
Whenever you felt the mood.
A scatty hostess with just-got-up
Bohemian style long blonde hair
Flying in all directions as you
Dance; playing air-guitar to the
Status Quo's 'Rocking' all over the World'.
That is how I will remember you.

Ten years earlier I recall you
Falling over yourself, eager to please
The customers at work. Always smiling,
Sometimes bewildered but so genuine,
Friendly and a little quirky.
Your hair was shorter and spiky
But you gave life everything
You had to offer: Yourself and your life.

Ten years later, I recall you
Falling over yourself, eager to please
The family and friends gathered
Around your hospital bedside.
Blonde hair fell in wispy clumps
Around your gaunt face.
You smiled at the jokes shared
That last evening;
It would have been too painful to laugh
Out loud. But you were my good friend
Of which I am extremely proud.
This is my story of my friend.

Debbie Perks

UNTIED NAVEL STRINGS

Faceless people on the move,
Walking, Walking, Walking for years.
Who are they? Where are they going?
When, Why and What are they looking for?

Faceless people in hooded cloaks,
Bare-footed, no mouth, no nose, just eyes,
Eyes, sad eyes, deceived eyes, wanting, haunted
Staring eyes, staring eyes, staring eyes.

Like refugees crossing a border
Some lonely, walking alone
Some holding hands helping each other,
Some of them carrying their sister, brother, half-sister, half-brother
Some of them holding their untrimmed navel string,
                                        that was never tied,
Some of them carrying their broken limbs
That were ripped from them so not to embarrass others

Faceless people, lots of people, millions of them,
Not taken by Famine, Disease, War madness or enemies
But brutality slaughter defencelessly by loved ones
Who chose, in the act of receiving or delivering their unformed bodies,
Who could have adopted them
To let those little eyes look up to love, affection and life?

Faceless people fighting back
Haunting, Haunting, Haunting.
Staring you straight in the face
When you are,
Sleeping, Sleeping, Sleeping.

Ken Draffin

AT THE EIFFEL TOWER

Our meeting chance
you wrapped me
in your green greatcoat

We walked white boulevards
clung to each other
deep in the city heart

Cuddled inside a small cafe
waiters smiled at us

At the Arc de Triomphe
you carried me in your arms
I warmed my hands beneath

your rough woollen clothes
we shared a baguette
I kept your red rose

Carole Luke

BITTER-SWEET REFRAIN

It started like this:
bliss simply wasn't the word for it -
we made each other laugh, shared things in common,
it was right at first sight . . .
making love exciting, erotic, romantic, tender in the night.
(wary, yes, both been hurt in the past)
but, you said you wouldn't be scarred forever
and, for now, just not to take things too fast.

Then, on New Year's Day (after your party)
you told me 'goodbye' had been on your mind -
but, I had somehow enticed you to stay,
besides, all that was in the past, and your desire for me confirmed
                                          you wanted things this way.

That day was one of my happiest
(it may sound 'corny' - but, true enough to say) -
but, then on St Patrick's Day you called me -
a relationship, after all, was not what you had in mind -
you wanted to be 'independent' - 'free' -
I knew without you it would be hard to smile again.

So, then, we sat and talked - though at first convention got
                                            the better of you,
balking at the suggestion we could be lovers without a name.

I told you, it was all the same to me,
Whatever we chose to call it -
we had a lot to gain - or more to lose that day
- if we threw it all away.

And, now, I'm dreaming of your touch again
(we've arranged to meet tomorrow)
a tale of bitter-sweet refrain
a story touched with joy and sorrow.

Maroushka Monro

JUST A HOUSEWIFE

Lonely! but what can I say?
No one will visit me today!
The sun is shining - I can't get out,
Oh dear! My knees! Doctor says - 'Just gout!'
Will pills prescribed put me right?
I'm hoping so, with all my might.
Weeds need pulling, washing needs doing,
When family come home, they'll want their pudding -
Will they wash up when crocks fill the sink?
No! Just rush to TV - what do you think?
I'm standing here with difficulty -
Washing up for the 'Hale and Hearty'!

Cindy White

ONE DEATH TOO MANY

She walked along the bank and asked to die.
No friends were there to help her in her plight.
The peaceful river flowed so slowly by.

She thought about her baby with a sigh.
The birth had filled her life with such delight.
She walked along the bank and asked to die.

Her child was ill, the voice so thin and high,
Her tiny face so pale, her form so slight.
The peaceful river flowed so slowly by.

The weeks went by and hope was running high.
But in the spring her baby lost the fight.
She walked along the bank and asked to die.

The little one was gone, severed the tie.
Shut out the day, admit the darkest night.
The peaceful river flowed so slowly by.

But life is costly and the price too high.
Her little boy came running into sight.
She walked along the bank and asked to die.
The peaceful river flowed so slowly by.

Dee Yates

THE PICTURESQUE

When the sun shines bright, and turns the mist away
And spring awakens, bringing the scented flower
When God sends down the light shower
Trees seem to whisper, as the leaves sway
We may picture the view, on a lovely day
As the waterfalls flow down the stream, yonder
Such peace is known, like a flowing river
That offers us hope in such a way

As we take a wish, or two and three
Or throw a coin, in the fountain, nearby
While, a traveller sketches the scenery
And paints the picturesque as birds fly
While, singing sweet phrases, upon a tree
Such wonders we view, and hear in the sky.

Jean P McGovern

MAGIC

Primrose was a fairy
Who lived in Bluebell Wood
She was kind to her friends
And always did good
One day all the animals
Found her very sad
What could have happened to make her feel so bad?
'I've broken my magic wand'
She told her little friends
It had to be mended before the day ends
They asked Wise Owl to help mend the wand
And took it back to Primrose who was sat by the pond
She picked it up and waved it in the air
Just missing the friends who were standing there
Whoosh! went the magic
Straight through the flowers
At last Fairy Primrose had back her powers.
She didn't notice that as her magic fell
It landed on an animal down in the dell
So what was the animal? I can hear you say
Well, it was the badger
That the magic touched that day.

(Badgers have a white stripe down their back)

Janis Smith

OUR PETS

They sit and listen to each word I say
And they seem to know the time of day
When it's time for their feed
They sit and whine
They seem to say 'It's our teatime.'
Three times a day they scratch and bark
They know it's time to go in the park
To lose these pets
We would be really sorry
One's a cross-Alsation
The other, a border collie.

C C Lee

HAPPY FAMILIES

Detached house in the country, her home was every housewife's dream,
The envy of her neighbours - things aren't always as they seem.
For no one saw the bruises, which lay beneath the skin,
And no one felt the hurt and anger festering within.

A pillar of society, a bank manager no less,
Investing and projecting, socialising with finesse.
But no one saw the 'family man' when he came home at night,
And no one heard the bitter words, the cruel taunts, the fights.

The children both had ponies and they both did well at school,
Which was surprising, since they lived within four walls of
gathering gloom,
But they played their CDs loudly, no one ever heard them weep,
And duvets pulled up over heads was how they liked to sleep.

Expensive double-glazing and a fourtrak on the drive,
A kitchen you would die for, but how could she stay alive?
Sunshine through the window, on the open cutlery drawer,
Sparkled on the bread knife - red drops splashed onto the floor.

A door slammed to behind her, cries of 'Throw away the key!'
A judge said 'Life!'
She shook her head and smiled,
'At last I'm free!'

Karen Hunton

PERSEVERANCE

Into a pail of milk two mice fell.
The one squeaked, panicked and was drowned.
The other did not let out a yell,
But started to swim round and round.

Round and around he steadily went
In pitch darkness, heart a-flutter,
Not really knowing what it all meant.
Came the dawn, he stood on butter.

Hywel Davies

CIRCLES OF LIFE

New life is found at springtime
perfectly formed, a babe so small
Ten tiny toes and fingers too
bright eyes and soft skin to recall.

Teeth to cut, first steps to take
chuckles of laughter we do hear.
Childhood days with school to attend
and holidays throughout the year.

Grow, work together each day
laugh and play for the world to see.
Adolescence and summer comes
then employment to find maybe.

Each hour learning things anew
precious moments with all to share.
As flowers reaching full their bloom
that someone special for to care.

Marriage, now a family
support through both good times and bad.
A slower lane, harvest to reap
more beautiful colours ne'er had.

Autumn glory brightly yields
good times with friends to cherish long
The years come and quickly go
love and memories keep us strong.

Leaves do fall, winter descends
retired, old age, death comes to all
Full circle life goes on and on
again Springtime with growth so small.

Margaret Jackson

ZODIAC REFLECTIONS:
A MIRROR IMAGE OF A HOT DATE

I feel so happy, I feel so free: I just want to be with that special 'he'.
We're going out tonight on a special hot date:
My heart is pounding so, I just can't wait: I just can't wait!
I just can't wait!

For I'm just a young and eager woman with a date at eight
And I just can't wait to see if my loved one will arrive on time!
And if it's true what he'll give to me: I'm so eager and full
of anticipation.

I'll have a nice long bath to make me giggle and laugh
Dreaming of all the sweet fun I'm going to have and give
As the water turns to temperature more cold: nothing will make me
less bold!
I cover myself with my latest perfume especially for my lover!
Smiling, beguiling, I pose in front of my looking-glass mirror
Slide on my newly-bought tights and examine my sights
For I'm sure to be on a winner, and maybe I'll shine like
a twinkling star!
Sparkling at every glimmer, my date arrives freshly just after eight!
I climb into his shiny car: my sweet perfume matches his
sexy aftershave
And we smile so sweetly together; ever such a joy to be with my lover.

For we're out for a rave, and we're feeling brave
And we prefer our romance sooner than later: I just can't wait!
He parks the car outside a moonlit bar, and we walk hand-in hand for a
glass or two: a happy interlude before the big feature!

I run so happily out of the moonlit bar
And jump so excitedly into the shiny car
My sign of the Zodiac is soon zooming in ecstasy so high
The warm air comes and goes, our two hearts beat
Really loving as one on the loving seat: Oh! Oh! Oh!
I feel so happy, I feel so free . . .
Exquisitely intertwined and intermingled in our own love heat
The setting being normal, and the occasion ever unique.

Oh! Oh! Oh! How it was worth going out on a fashion-spending spree
For my sign of the Zodiac was as sweetly high as it ever could be
A kiss for you, a kiss for me, Oh! Oh! Oh! I feel so happy,
$$\text{I feel so free!}$$

Jackie J Docherty

A DOG'S LIFE

A bright brown eye appears,
just one;
too much too soon would never do.
False alarm, revert to standby;
snoozing through the afternoon.

Remote commotion,
action stations;
ears erect, the loose fur flies.
Stroking, patting, high emotions;
reciprocated love from man's best friend.

Time to curl up on the sofa,
let the day slide slowly by.
Heavy lids closed tightly,
life goes on;
dreams of a bone.

Ian Stewart

WAR GAMES

'Bang! You're dead!'
'Bang, bang! And you!'
Screams, cries and falling bodies
Fill the floor, a smell of fear
Lingers lightly, swept aside
Carelessly with handclaps
- Silence arriving shiftily
Small shuffling, scuffing shoes,
'Nursery's finished, home you go,'
Little children learning.

'In we go boys!'
Giddy gallants, guys misguided,
Bullets raping virgin bodies,
Blood's odour camouflaging fear,
Dignity and conscience swept aside,
Missiles shriek like cowardly bats,
Blind - deadly accurate,
Mangled limbs leave empty shoes,
Battle's won, trembling hero's home,
Little learnt by children.

Brenda Dove

PAINTING

How oft I would have liked a picture to see,
But whilst at work doodling and sketching had to satisfy me.
You see all that is needed is a light pencil and pad.
Easily used during the short breaks that I had.
But I had loved colour all of my life
So when I first retired with paint I was rife.
Not in the garish way, it is often seen,
But with an eye for detail and depicting a lovely scene.
I was looking around the other day,
And realised that things from the natural world held sway.
I remember painting articles and people too,
But of these, I noticed, I'd kept only a few.
One of my proudest possessions is of a tiger at night,
Drooling in the silvery moonlight.
There is plenty of colour too
Intermingled with the different shades of blue.

Betty Green

WOOLLY BITE

My boyfriend found
A quiet place where
'Midst wondrous' scenery
Trout fishing, hobby to share.

On river bank, knitting sat I
Gazing into waters below
Wondering if
Fish to watch, or woolly grow.

Suddenly, wool ball, unwinding rolled in
Entangling line, hook, fish.
Horrified, in went woolly needles too.
Catching, fat trout for tasty supper dish.

My boyfriend no more,
I cannot swim,
Going along to supermarket soon
For 'sardines in a tin'.

Ivy Lott

THE ISLE OF SHELLS
(Dedicated to Laura Z)

First trip away from home, excited but nervous too
Waves goodbye and kisses . . . remember 'I love you'
A week away together, so crowded but so alone
'Cos thoughts drift unexpected to thoughts of Mum and home.
Sleeping bags unfolded, all share the big white tent
Chores to be completed then postcards can be sent.
Idle childish chatter, days spent on the beach
Grown-ups try to organise (and occasionally teach!)
Groups of little children gather round rock pools
Look for crabs and fishes, relaxing of school rules.

Suddenly . . . a child is missing: Tiny, blonde hair (long)
Everybody searching, oh where can she be gone?
Coastguards' help is summoned, there seems an endless wait
Search with expectation but fear an awful fate
Sirens in the distance the roar of rotor blade
Searching ever-searching, the place where children played.
At last the child is spotted way out upon the sea
A scream and pointing hands all fear her destiny
Snatched from sea's strong clutches, dragged away from wave
Expert medical knowledge, hope that they can save
Crowds all nervous waiting for the gathering on the sand
At last step back exhausted, showing only tiny hand.

Beautiful little girl, wet hair long and gold
Fragile body taken only ten years old.
Placed in helicopter, rose into the sky
People bowed their heads and asked one question . . . Why?
Cool sunny day in August school trip down to the sea
Laughter, fun and happiness all end in tragedy.

But happy now forever as round the beach she trails
On the Isle of Shells, Tremadog Bay in Wales.

Rianne Cannon

JACKO'S HOLIDAY

Jacko went out one summer day
Up on the hills and far away;
Down through the woods so quiet and cool,
Down to a farm beside a pool.

> Along the farmyard past carts and trucks
> Into the water went drakes and ducks;
> Little brown ducklings by three and four
> Followed their parents away from the shore.

They looked at the dog in a menacing way,
So Jacko decided he'd better not stay.
And giving a bark which implied, 'I don't care,'
He went off through the gate with his head in the air.

> He trotted along for nearly a mile,
> Till he saw in the hedge a grey stone stile.
> With a squeeze and a wriggle he crept beneath,
> And found himself out on the wide green heath.

Here he could scamper and roll and play,
With no one to tell him to go away.
Up on the hillocks and down in the hollows,
With no one to see except skylarks and swallows.

> Jacko went hunting for rabbits or rats,
> Played with some puppies and barked at some cats,
> Ate half a biscuit and buried a bone,
> And found an old ball which he took for his own.

Jacko came home when the sunset was red,
Ate up his dinner and crept into bed,
And soon he was dreaming, as little dogs may,
Of all the events of his little dog's day.

Kathleen M Hatton

COOK-IN-CHARGE

Take heed, good listener, to my tale of conflict, clash and quarrel
And let me tell of what befell, then memorise the moral!
Some years ago, as the story goes, down at the old Day Centre,
Came a new recruit, all coy and cute, Employment Office sent her.
She took the job they offered her; allow me to enlarge:
They saw no harm in one with charm, so they called her
                                        'Cook-in-Charge'.
But what they never knew or guessed or saw in nightmare fancy,
Was, hour by hour, the growing power, the subtle necromancy!
The Cook-in-Charge took charge indeed and this now was the upshot,
The 'feeder' fancied being 'leader' so turned into a despot.

Quartermaster of the kitchen, Prima Donna of the show,
The Empress with the dishmop, the Generalissimo!

'Eat your biscuits galley slaves, for they're an extra treat,
Of course there's weevils in 'em . . . they supplement the meat.
No, you can't have ice-cream, sit down, shut up, I'm boss,
Don't start, who *do* you think you are? You're warned.
                                          I'm getting cross!'

Now this must be the moral and it's one to take to heart,
Look carefully at your candidate and question from the start.
Yes, ask about her cooking and her knowledge of nutrition,
But delve a little deeper into personal ambition.
All too late they saw it, the truth so clear and large;
How they wished they'd never done it, called the lady
                                        'Cook-in-Charge'.

Kathy Twist

IN HARMONY

It's the end of term and they come with their folders full
Granny has to look at everything that has been done at school
Writing, sums, drawings and paintings, so much to look through
Then they all wait for appraisal which in most cases was due
Wall space is running out so most of last year's work will come down.
Of course some will remain especially pictures of parrot and clown.
Little hands are eager to help and from the drawer comes blu-tack
Granny carefully fixes all new paintings up, for that she has
                                                                  a knack.
A little patience, love and encouragement brings the best out in us all
Everyone is happy now; and just look at that lovely colourful wall!

Margaret Cowan

DUNKIRK: A CHILD'S EYE VIEW

Somehow I heard about Dunkirk.
Was it on the wireless?
Probably not -
'Careless talk costs lives',
but I got to know.

There was a call put out
for small ships, small boats, sail boats, yachts,
pleasure boats, river boats, fishing boats, ferries,
anything that could float,
could put to sea,
could pick up men from beaches.

And so they went
out of Sussex, out of Kent,
from the sea towns and the rivers
at least as far as the Mersey
and certainly from the Thames.

They went like thieves
to seize what was already their own.
They stole out of English harbours
and left for Dunkirk.

I saw pictures of the men coming back
on the Movietone News.
For the first time
I was aware of being English.

And then France fell -
a lesson in geography
a shift of emotion.
The message came dramatically.
Something was closing in.

Pam Redmond

DISTURBANCE

The throbbing of music invades the air
Played without thought or any care
Disturbing the peace of a winter's night
Giving the elderly quite a fright
The young do not care for peace and quiet
They are more concerned with causing a riot
They shout and they scream, then they rave
But singly they are not very brave
They band together to get high on drugs
That nice lad next door is suddenly a thug
And on the way to utter ruin
He wonders if he has enough glue in
Then comes the day he does not wake up
The rest of the crowd get quite a shock
The funeral is held, the mourning is done
But they are all soon back on the 'crack' run
So let us pity them all for they are insane
Let loose in the world without a brain.

Margaret Gurney

TRUE STORY: IN A FLAP!

'I'm off to the shop' my wife announced to me.
'Hang on a tick, I'll keep you company.'
Off we set, closing our new front door,
Looking at it with some pride
I could have fallen through the floor!
I'd left my keys inside!
With a look of disbelief and fear
My wife said 'How do we get back in?'
'Don't worry my dear! I've got the back door key,'
I said with a cheeky grin.
With some relief, we went round to the back,
But relief soon turned to anger!
You have to get to the back door through the porch,
And I realised, I'd dropped a clanger!
The porch was locked!
Through the frosty silence, I said with a cry
'I'll get through the dog flap, it's 29 inches high!
If our big dog can get in, so can I!'
Now, the dog flap is down an alley, between
                    conservatory and porch,
It's only a 14-inch gap, and I have a 40-inch paunch!
But, bravely I sidled along, and dropped down on my side
Got stuck, like a human wedge, 'I guess I was too wide'
'While you're down there' laughed the wife, 'take this stick
Put your arm through the hole, unhook the window quick!'
After fiddling around (for I couldn't see) the window opened.
                                        Good for me!
My wife hopped through, opened the door,
Leaving me lying on the floor.
'What about me?' I said, feeling like a mutt,
'Sorry, Love, you are on your own, I'm off, before the shops shut'
I can see the headlines now - *'Pensioner in the Doghouse'*.

K Pusey

SAND OF RED

Sands to conquer, sands of red.
For fellow men's lives to give, of sand scorched with,
blood of tyranny for man to save his fellow men,
of landing craft, on rivers of blood.

Sands of tyranny to save they do,
from sands of red scorched with blood of fellow men,
on those foreign shores, from tyranny they have seen
of life being spent so young and so old of youth.

Sands of red scorched with blood,
they do and did, yet it was peace they wanted of this land
scorched with blood of fellow men for times of peace,
they did give their all on that foreign land.

From a life of tyranny that was fought
to remember them of this new century blood, so young.
Sand of red scorched with blood from tyranny they did fight.
Life so young they did give.

In youth eternal, sand of red foreign shore,
they did conquer life so short, they did give for fellow
men, they did save from that shore.
Sand of red.

Of that D-Day landing on that shore
this Anniversary to remember of youth so young yet
Not old, that they did give for peace
everlasting, they did fight!

From a life of tyranny, they did give,
in time of war, to be no more of this century new.
No sand of red to be fought of youth so young
Yet not old.

Of this D-Day landing to remember
those who did give on those of a foreign shore.

A May

FIRST MEETING

She had spoken to him only once on the phone,
Told her he was not married and lived alone.
She had said she was slender aged twenty-four,
He was slightly older than her and six feet-four.
They had arranged to meet outside a large store in town,
Old-fashioned shop, with window casings painted brown.

At two-thirty that day they had chosen to meet,
To help her keep calm she chewed another soft sweet.
She was a little early and paced up and down,
Causing a bit of a stir in her floral gown.
Suddenly a well-dressed man appeared in sight,
And then found conversing with him seemed just right.

All too soon he had to leave and they had to part,
But he took away with him a piece of her heart.
Now they both felt sure they had met their soulmate,
Agreed to meet that evening, for no need to wait.
As she walked the long way home her heart skipped a beat,
Regained her composure sat on a park seat.

S Mullinger

BUTTERFLIES

Small and elegant,
their tiny stained-glass windows
pound the solid air,
each pulse an endless battle
against the powerful but,
seemingly empty space.

They ride upon the wind's waves,
high and low,
diving then soaring far into the
heavenly sky.

They daintily dance around
in this water-colour,
showing off their miniature rainbows,
looking for a flower that
takes their fancy.
Or an occasional head is
picked as a landing pad
for these silken helicopters.

As the warm yellow slowly
slips from the picture,
they frantically flutter
searching for a
place to rest their
precious materials.
The darkness falls and
these amazing creatures
can finally relax until
the lazy dawn breaks again.

Sophie Cara Nicolaysen (15)

THE STORY OF SILVER

Sitting on my shoulder, eating nuts fed by our hands,
Silver loved to chatter and I swear he'd understand,
Every single word we said, he'd fix us with his eyes,
His favourite words were 'chocolate', 'sweets'
                             and 'steak and kidney pies.'

Silver loved exploring and this really sealed his fate,
He'd leave us via the cat flap and he'd not come back till late;
The neighbours knew and loved him, though their
                             patience would wear thin,
Especially when he chose to take his food from full dustbins.

Silver was a genius and he didn't miss a thing,
He stopped me getting bullied and he found Mum's wedding ring.
He knew when we were angry, he would hide beneath the chair
And cry for hours and hours till he made my Mum despair.

We all have our weaknesses, but Silver's was to climb,
It's quite unfair he paid the price upon his very first time.
The pylon looked to be quite safe, but as our friend found out,
It wasn't . . . electric currents kill, without a trace of doubt.

Silver had a funeral, once his body had been found
Tail up and body stiff, lying on the ground . . .
Silver, I will miss you, you were quite a special friend
And that's the story of Silver, but it isn't quite the end.

I wanted to remember Silver, so had his body stuffed;
When finished, he looked fantastic . . . his perfect tail puffed . . .
He'll always be beside me, even though he's now deceased;
Silver the Squirrel had a life and now he'll rest in peace.

Lisa-Marie Corcoran

My Beautiful Day

Get up! Get up! The sun calls down.
My feet answer the call.
They spring onto the carpet, into my shoes,
Down the stairs and into the hall.
With morning paper and morning tea
I settle down to read, the news, the scandal,
All there for me to see.
What's this? I turn quickly away
For what I see I know will spoil
My beautiful day.
A bear caged so tightly it can't lift its head.
It is pleading 'Let me out, let me out' he said.
The photographer taking one last look,
Walked away from the bear feeling
Pleased with his scoop.
Tears rolled down my cheeks
This can't be true, can it?
What can I do?
Don't think I say; but I do.

Audrey Bowden

BANTER AT HER MAJESTY'S GATE WALTON

'Good morning, Miss Smith, education'
'Any identification?'
'Yes'
'Of course, you come every Thursday, don't you?'
'Yes'
'Think, it's worth it?
(Silence)
They'll teach you a thing or two, better watch out
(Silence)
German, is it?'
'Yes'
*'Makes me laugh that, foreign languages in here
A waste of ratepayers' money
They have their own lingo, as it is
Never taught us anything like that in school
Discipline, yes
Headmaster's cane
Good, sharp, no nonsense discipline'*

'Stop!

Watch out your automatic door doesn't jam
One of them might slip through
And shoot you

And another thing
I am teaching them to fly

But don't tell anyone, will you?'

Alfa

MING'S EVENING OUT

Alarm bells split the air, tyres screech on tarmac,
Hastily clad firemen, explode out of engines,
With hoses unreeling, yards down the street.

Buildings and vehicles, now blazing with gusto,
Heated mirages caper, smoke devils dance,
Fire seriously settling, burning and consuming.

Water jetting skywards, falling with precision,
Swallowed by smoke, slowly dampening down,
Sooty black figures fight, knowing they will win.

White helmets nods knowingly, yes it's arson!
Meat distribution company, it was the target.
Animal rights saboteurs, are they the culprits?

Ermingtrude Smith, prefers to be called Ming,
Driving to work, views last evening's havoc,
A smile of satisfaction, beams all over her face.

Last evening's party, mission accomplished,
No one will think about barbecues today!
Roast pork and gammon steaks,
        Won't be on the menu tonight!

Jean Wearn Wallace

THE HARP

While sitting on my cloud one day,
practising my harp,
through lack of concentration
I played D flat and not D sharp.
The Heavenly Choir was not amused.
I could tell from their frosty glare,
so I floated off to do my own thing
and arrived at a flight of stairs.
I descended the deep stairwell
and knocked upon a door.
It was answered by a man in red,
who said I was welcome there.
There was a strong smell of sulphur
And the air seemed very hot.
I asked if I'd have to play my harp.
He said that I would not,
Greatly relieved, I followed him
as he showed me what to do.
I'm happy stoking the furnace now
and my harp still looks brand new.

Carole Revell

HIDE AND SEEK!

I hear the sound at dead of night -
Rotor blades' loud whirring, whirring -
Sleeping folk are stirring, stirring.
The deafening noise is overhead:
I spring quickly out of bed - it's
A helicopter - what a sight!

Its brilliant white beam pinpoints down,
Dancing briefly o'er ageing thatch,
O'er roofs of slate, o'er tiles that match -
O'er grotesque shapes and boundary walls,
O'er jet black gardens, large and small -
In daylight - painted green, or brown.

Hovering above our narrow road,
Police inside are watchful, seeking -
Muttering sounds - though rarely speaking;
Closely following that beam of light,
Piercing the darkness of the night.
Have villains sought some fresh abode?

'Copter's gone 'twould not have landed!
Beaming searchlight's soon extinguished -
Noisy whirring sound's diminished.
To carry on's a waste of time:
Elsewhere fly, to fight fresh crime - thus -
Hunters all, leave empty handed.

Glan Grey Jones

OUR TRUE LOVE

The first time I saw her, was at a dance,
We fell in love, at our first glance.
After we had courted, for six months or more,
I was invited, through her front door.
Part of her Family, I was soon to become,
Her parents treated me, like a son.
Then on our wedding day,
Her proud father, gave her away.
That night, as we cuddled, kissed and had fun,
A pregnant woman, she had become.
In the Maternity Ward, she gripped my hand,
Our baby was due, which we had planned.
As the hours slowly passed by,
She pushed and screamed, and began to cry,
Then our first baby has arrived.
At home we had everything prepared,
To give our baby, every love and care.
Our parents visited us, on most days,
We were guided by what, they had to say.
After all those pains, my wife had gone through,
She decided, she would love two.
Life was tough, we both worked hard,
Gave them both, all the love we had.
After they left school, and found a profession,
Romance would soon become their intentions.
At our Golden Wedding, as we danced,
We both remembered, our first glance.

Brian Marshall

Marrakech Movies

On time we reached that appointed spot
Where we were to start a little trot
Through the town in a carriage and pair
Thirteen, or fourteen, were waiting there.

We all had our Sunday best dress on
And were soon setting off, on our run
We cantered alone in one long file
Nothing to see for many a mile.

One driver dared to make a quick dash
Although this action was rather rash,
He lost part of a wheel in the rush
Which caused a cheer from the rest of us.

We all slowed down, the repair was done
Watching it proved to be such good fun
They stuck the tyre back and nailed it on
I said a prayer to the Holy One.

Our journey's end came into view
At the edge of a long avenue
Of market stalls all selling their ware,
A low down cafe was waiting there.

We sipped mint tea, which was much too sweet
Watched by the locals out in the street,
Homeward, we led in front of the rest.
I just hoped his carriage was the best.

Auntie called 'Stop, let us be last
It is upsetting me travelling fast.'
Plea unheeded, first back to the base,
Relief all round, for the end of race.

Margaret Whitaker

GRAND PRIX

As the chequered flag fell, each man ran for his car!
Mid the roar of great engines - tyres screamed hard on the tar!
We went off down the straight, in a deafening stampede;
Each man's aim, at the outset - to get in the lead!

Swinging into the bends, smoothly changing the gears,
While keeping the 'Revs' up - ignoring the cheers!
Superchargers a-whining; lube oil heating up fast;
And the car just ahead - was the one to get past!

As the laps numbered sharply, I put in my bid,
Then the car in front swerved - and was caught in a skid!
I swung hard on the wheel, first to left, then to right;
I just missed him by inches - it gave me a fright!

Soon my nerves re-adjusted; my foot went down hard;
I'd avoided collision - without being scarred!
It was time for my pit stop, for I had to re-fuel;
My tyres were all changed - while I drank something cool!

I returned to the race, gaining lap after lap;
Only one car in front and I narrowed the gap!
With a last burst of speed, I shot past him - to win!
Drove a *Victory Lap* - trying hard not to grin!

For the race I'd just won - with phenomenal speed,
Made me World Champion Driver - by a clear six point lead!
Soon the crowd round the platform, would shortly feel rain
As I shook up the Magnum - which gushed with champagne!

Ron Bissett

THE GLADEYE

Old gladeye looks at the sky
as rose-coloured clouds bury her mind
a time so long ago has passed her by
now a pale reflection in her eyes.

Old gladeye sees what she wants to see
her golden haze blocks out the darkness
that covered a land with fears
hidden under a veil of tears.

Look at me and not the sun
for the world looks on and sighs
can you not see the reality
or does your memory ease with lies?

Old gladeye turns her gaze
to the picture old and brown
finally tears clear the clouds
and only now she sees.

As her gaze looks down
he smiles up at her gladeye.

Colin Skilton

AND FINALLY EMPATHY

'Did we give birth to that?
Maybe in his teens he could be good.'
But teens are notorious.
We shouldn't list his misdemeanours
But they're so copious, loyalty fails.
Well, what did he do today?'
The Mum, with drooping mouth and haggard eyes
Pleads 'Oh, only smashed another neighbour's window.'

His vigour and intensity of life
Disregards the norm
Swashbuckling every day.
And shaking parents, though reluctant,
Admire his total courage,
Uncomprehending, lack of fear.

Teenage years passed
Some spark of care ignited
And manhood finds him
A wondrous brave enlightened leader
Devoid of self concern or self esteem
Loading his parents with pride
And gentle solace for their very lives.
Strange now to think how he was
Hauled screaming from the womb.

Vie Tulloch

INTERVIEW

Waiting anxious moments pass
Notes twisted in an gnarled hand
Come in do, are you too
A candidate for the interview?

Clasped, tight-skinned, fistful of money
Questions on The Times or Guardian
Newspapers from 1968 to the present day
The interview is in progress.

Clothes horse, model proportions
Hair falling over the left shoulder
Details, single, able to work
Interview quite an experience.

S M Thompson

THE BOMBS

Patrick and Michael went out for a walk
Down a lane in the green countryside.
When, all of a sudden, they stopped in their tracks.
Something strange in the grass they espied.

They looked at each other but said not a word
As they prodded and poked all around.
Then all of a sudden they knew what it was -
Three bombs (unexploded) they'd found.

They knew it was risky. There was no other choice.
Said one, 'Well, we'd better be quick,'
So they got a wheelbarrow and loaded them on
To carry them down to the nick.

They were walking along when Pat suddenly said,
'What if one should explode 'fore we're through?'
'Oh, if that should occur,' old Michael replied,
'We'll tell 'em we only found two!'

W I Cooksey

She Hides Her Children

She hides her children
From the Nazi regime,
For she knows what will come
Is not her mind's dream.

She hides her children
From the future of camps,
For she knows they will come
At night with their lamps.

She hides her children
From his boys in brown shirts,
For she knows they will come
And that's what really hurts.

She hides her children
She has only three,
For she knows they will come
And it won't help to plea.

Marcus Tyler

THE POOL

Through summer woods at dawn, a shadow slips:
a prince with ivory skin and crimson lips,
his cape is midnight-blue, pure white the steed he rides;
silent, between the trees, the horse and rider glide.
They reach at last a quiet forest glade
where sunlight fairies dance, a stream cascades
over smooth stones and down into a pool
of sparkling water, crystalline and cool.

The prince dismounts, completely unaware:
he cannot feel the magic in the air.
A lissom naiad rises from the water
and weaves a spell: a nymph's mercurial laughter,
mingled with the scent of early morn,
a whisper of the breeze, the mist at dawn,
the smell of dew on moss, the fresh green leaves,
these, then, are the threads she takes and weaves
into an enchantment. Still the prince
gazes at the pool. Unseen, the nymphs
wait in the water. Enchanted, then, he stands
and walks into the pool, their outstretched hands
pull him down into their home beneath
the waterfall, in hidden caverns deep.

The mare returns alone, bedraggled, lame,
she's cast a shoe, has knots in tail and mane.
Back in the palace many a story's told
of beauteous nymphs who live in waters cold,
of forest glades, enchanted waterfalls:
dark tales. Secure behind strong walls
the courtiers do not lose a moment's sleep.
And yet, they say, one maid was heard to weep.

Gwyneth Box

THE FERRYMAN

Through all the storms and tempests is come this fine day,
I am here, waiting by the riverside for my passengers to come by.
I cast my eye abroad, over the river to where another land does lie,
Lies in wait for all the world to make it their welcoming home.
Tired from their pilgrimage, I seat my guests most
                             comfortably on board my boat.
We float through the silver and the gold of the water flowers.
In the field we left behind, the horse ruffles his mane and
                             nuzzles the feathers of the grass,
Lifting his head to view his domain and gently surveys our progress.
Bees drone, birds sleep in their midsummer siesta.
My guests repose on silken cushion smiling at the
                             blue and green as we sail into the sun.
Emerging below the castle walls, where friends and loved
                                         ones welcome us home
With song and laughter that banish long lost pain.
Was it so brief a time since I ferried them?
How pleased I was that I made them unafraid for their journey
to accomplish on this summer's day.
No illusion this, but the truth, for truth and love make
beautiful things out of truthful and loving thoughts.
Thoughts are the truth, and loving thoughts bring beauty
to heal the tired spirit.
Born out of love, not pain, but in ease.
Blue day, green God of the Universe reigns, with
                             light God of air and water,
We acknowledge your power, the power from whence you came.
So I stand free, and to cross this crystal channel,
No soul will I have pay me.
Do not close thine eyes with cold coin, for his pleasure is mine.
His love is my love for all of you, that conveys you
                             across this watery bridge,
Through the gateway towards the birthright that is thine.

Susan Kemp

A Priceless Friendship

The Owl and the Pussycat charged . . .
The light brigade (and the gas)
To their little plastic credit card . . .
Payment made, efficient, fast.

Pussy thought . . . 'All cards are cool'
The wise old Owl said, *'No'*
He told his friend, 'You are a fool,'
So Pussy said . . . 'I'll *go.*'

If . . . I had kept my head, Puss thought . . .
I would have bread and honey . . .
Or a bit of fish . . . I could have bought.
Had I not 'give up' on money.

Hoo cried old Owl, hoo . . . hoo . . . hoo
Would give cash for a plastic purse.
Hee hoo gives cash and friendship too . . .
Will find that he is cursed.

We'll have to sell the pea green boat
Then go to live in 'Jumbly land.'
Oh weh! For the joys of a five pound note
And the paw of friendship in my hand.

Money isn't enough, poor Pussy groaned,
To make up for friendship . . . all gone wrong.
I would give . . . anything I owned,
For Owly's friendship . . . warm and strong.

So Owl and Pussy . . . both sad and wise
Behaved as good friends should.
They laughed and wept . . . then dried their eyes,
And . . . they promised . . . to be good.

Brenda Robson-Eifler

ENDLESS DESERTS

The boy,
The shop,
The toys,
The endless toys,
Colours mixing together to make a rainbow of multicoloured toys.

In awe was the boy,
Never had he seen so many!
Towering over him,
Like the ancient pillars of Rome.
Old ones,
New ones,
Expensive ones,
Cheap ones.

The boy liked coming here,
The endless sun beating down on him like in the endless deserts.
The deep blue skies drifting on forever.

He could visit his favourite place whenever he wanted,
As all he had to do . . .
Was close his eyes . . .

Thomas Harrison (13)

THE HAPPENING

I had often walked along that street
Cobbled road beneath my feet.
Narrow pavements winding up,
Old shops and houses scarely wide
Pushed together side by side.

It was a grey and sunless day,
As I wandered on my way
When I saw built in a wall,
An ancient wood and iron door
That I had never spied before.

As I looked it opened wide
An old man beckoned me inside.
I crossed the busy winding lane
And stepped into the dingy hall,
Dust and cobwebs wall to wall.

My eyes soon saw through the gloom
As we walked from room to room.
From floor to ceiling in every space
A wondrous sight made me stare.
The house was filled with antiques rare.

He said 'I wish these things to sell.
Choose what you wish, the price then I'll tell.
You are a man of taste and charm
And will wisely choose
I promise this, you will not lose.'

I had no money, I could not buy.
So thanked him kindly and with a sigh
Turned and left the house.
But thought of treasures left behind
And tried hard not to care or mind.

All night upon my bed I tossed.
Dreamed of strange chances lost.
Next morn I rose and borrowed funds.
Back to Lincoln in great haste,
Along the country roads I chased.

Up the streets I quickly ran,
But no sight of the grey old man,
Nor the door within the wall.
Along the road I searched in vain,
But no sign of either did I find again.

Jenni A Rose

IF ONLY

If only I could return
To the season of my spring,
His advances would not spurn,
A different tune I would sing.

If only I could undo
All the wrongs I committed,
As informative years flew,
Monetary dues frittered.

If only, a phrase well used,
That I say over again,
Moments of choice I abused,
Causing others and me strain.

If only then I had known,
How the future would unfold,
Other seeds I would have sown,
Whilst fresh, enigmatic, bold.

If only, yet looking back
To my immaturity,
Life's wisdom I was in lack,
Accured by each *if only*.

If only I could pass on,
The knowledge suffering gains;
My fledged cygnet, now a swan,
Has her own *if only* pains.

Janet Hewitt

WASTED YEARS

I don't pretend to know everything,
I've no idea what the future holds.
I can't anticipate what tomorrow will bring,
I can only wait to see what unfolds.

I can't say if there's a God above
Or if we possess immortal souls.
I'm not an expert when it comes to love,
I've never set ambitious goals.

There is much I've failed to understand
And many things I've yet to see.
The days rarely work out as planned,
It's the way life's meant to be.

And yes, I harbour a few regrets,
I've been a prisoner of my fears.
But time will pass and I'll forget
The memories of wasted years.

Alan Palmer

PARENTS

My father died when I was five
And it was very sad
As I have had to go through life
Without a loving dad.

My mother did her very best
With nine children in her nest
I was the last one to arrive
And entered life with overdrive.

My memories of my dad are few
For he had his own point of view
A strict parent without a doubt
You did not dare to scream or shout.

His role in life was to make sure
That we were fed and clothed though poor
He worked hard on a building site
Carrying a hod which wasn't light.

To his workplace I would go
Taking his lunch he had no time to slow
I think the worry and the strife
Helped to end his shortened life.

Mum carried on regardless
And gave us all she had
My brothers said that I was spoilt
This used to make me mad.

For very soon they all left home
And I was left there on my own
Always at my mother's heels
I know how an only child feels.

Raised with morals and respect
My mother did her level best.

Winifred Tutte

THE DAY I SAW THE ECLIPSE - 11TH AUGUST 1999

We gathered on that August day in 1999,
All with our special viewers so we would not harm our eyes,
Blue skies had deserted us, and thick cloud hid the Sun,
But we numbered several hundred, and were determined to have fun.
On Cornwall's rocky Lizard Point, we watched Day turn into Night,
Then right on cue, through parted clouds, we saw a marvellous sight,
The diamond ring and Bailey's beads, the Corona, we saw them all,
People were screaming, strangers were hugging,
We were all held in its thrall.
All too soon it raced away, other lands were waiting,
We were left all excited, thrilled and celebrating.
Calm returned, and we climbed down and went our separate ways,
But we had shared in something special,
We will remember all our days.

Patricia Jones

SURPRISES

Every day is a new surprise.
It may be small, it may be large,
But whatever its value it is still a surprise.
Last week I had two offers,
Both I found fit to refuse.
One had been often repeated,
The other was panic related,
But neither one did I regret.

Last week, instead of shopping,
I sat in a pew in the Church.
I lit a candle for someone
And waited for calm to ensue.
Then, sadly, I visited Beau Vista,
The old family home about to be sold.
I let the peace of my childhood
Flow through my veins.
I realised it wasn't the place
But the people that mattered,
So goodbye was easier to say.

Today, someone came unexpected,
Whom I thought a hundred miles distant.
His presence restored my vitality,
Hence this poem has now been created.
After a blank of two years hiatus,
I find I can write once again
And that surprise is to me,
The most wondrous gift of them all.

Mary Marriott

WE BOUGHT A HOUSE

We went into the office to sign up
Right on the old dotted line
For we'd just bought a house up in Wiltshire
Will they think we are out of our minds?

Now the details said 'some work needed'
But we'll manage to fix that alright
'Cause we'll get some good local labour
They said it would take a fortnight.

Oh the noise and the dust they created
With floorboards ripped up in the hall
And wires sticking out of the ceilings
And plaster all wet on the walls.

Now just as we thought we had finished
An alarm they decided to fix
But to clear it you just have to hurry
As you only have 45 ticks.

We woke up quite early next morning
And went down to make cups of tea
When the peace of the morning was shattered
Like the start of the next world war 3.

Now the noise the alarm had created
Sent the neighbours all ridged with fright
And I broke the best cups and saucers
Now the cat, in the head's, not quite right.

Elizabeth Hudson

STOLEN CHERRIES

My first visit was as a pilgrim,
To Washington DC, in awe
Where cherry blossom full abounds,
With beauty's odourless perfume.

I walked white blossomed streets and parks,
With loss of breath withdrawn from me,
Such quantity of magnificence,
Fresh bloomed each year, greets reborn spring.

My mind was seized by memories
Of England, Land where I was born,
There stood upright outside our door,
Just one fruit-bearing Cherry tree.

We welcomed blossom's pleasant shade,
Protected fruit as best we could.
From birds attempted steal of fruit,
No need, with yield enough for all.

Dreamily I wandered engrossed,
Oblivious of else around.
When fast, like strong whirlwind, was snatched,
My briefcase, I thought held secure.

I gave good chase, could not compete,
With stride much younger than my own,
Gone were both cash and documents,
Effects I'd worked hard to achieve.

Meandering thoughts did quick return,
To fruits upon sole Cherry tree,
Of how I stood those hungry birds,
From rights more crucial than of mine.

Perhaps this human seizing bird,
With thin shape that matched famine's form
Had greater need for what he snatched,
To feed his chicks and save his nest.

Complacently there let matter rest.

Leslie Fine

LAMBO

A sheepish look upon his face,
rows of bullets across his chest,
This sheep's name was Lambo,
and he was known to be the best.
A .45 Magnum was his favourite 'piece',
kept neatly hidden beneath his fleece.
He worked for a firm named 'Sheepsafe Inc',
sniffing out wolves by their evil stink.
Now Lambo's partner was 'Dirty Larry',
he too was tough as mutton,
He'd take on wolves, and foxes too,
for battles he was a glutton.
Alas, the wolves found a different weapon,
One to change old Lambo's course.
No longer did wolves stand and fight,
They simply howled 'Mint sauce, mint sauce.'
Soon things were back to normal,
Back to Mother Nature's way,
Where the wolves hold all the aces,
and lambs run and bleat all day.

Duncan C Callander

My Mate Charlie

Come and meet my mate Charlie,
He'll show you a good time.
Come and meet my mate Charlie,
So what if it's a crime?
He'll take you on a journey,
The trip will blow your mind.
But just watch out, have care, take heed,
Do you really know what you're going to find?

The choice is made, the deed is done,
You grasp at Charlie's hand and start to run.
Your throat is dry, it's turning numb.
Your mind shouts out, 'What have I done?'
Then the buzz, the joy, the high,
The feelings you hope will never die.
The pinnacle of pleasure, the peak of perfect bliss,
The rush of adrenaline,
Oh life was made for this!

You turn to smile at Charlie, and realise he's not there.
The smile fades and is replaced with a feeling of despair.
A deep desolation fills your soul
And down you disappear into a big black hole.
Charlie's laughing at you, while all you feel is pain.
He's no mate of yours,
His friendship is no gain.

Julia Pattison

DRAGON FROM HELL

'*My* teacher has a better shout
Than *your* teacher!'
My little brother said one day -
But when he told my dad, he said,
'I'll tell you this tale if I may . . .
Son, there once was a teacher
Mostly greatly revered,
When she opened her mouth,
Her whole *face* disappeared.
Her shout was enormous,
It wobbled the ceiling,
And all of the kids
Got that sinking feeling
In the pit of their stomachs -
They sat in a spell,
Entranced by that monster
The *Dragon From Hell!*
You'd better believe me
For if one should snigger,
Her shout would get bigger, and bigger,
And *bigger*!
She hollered so much
It was just as we feared,
Her jaw gaped so wide
That her *head* disappeared.
So writhing and screaming
She fell to the floor . . .
'Oh help me, *please* help me,'
That miss did implore.
We sent for a doctor
Who came and he said
*'I think your class teacher
Is quite off her head . . .
She's dead!'*

Kendric Ross

A Child Of The Thirties

Raised in the thirties
Before a horrific war,
She survived blitzed forties,
Witnessed an atomic roar.

Wedded bliss in the fifties,
Three children soon to follow,
One born spastic and retarded,
Resulting in great sorrow!

Offspring rewarded her
Two grandsons came her way,
Happy millennium pensioner
Awaits a golden wedding day!

Pat Heppel

THE PARK

Through all her life she loved the park
In every changing clime.
The joy of budding trees in spring
Their fragrant summer time.
The autumn glow of ripened leaves
In wind whirled pirouettes.
The winter cloak which softly left
Snow covered silhouettes.

Her heart would lift in wondrous peace.
This was her paradise.
For nature's magic all around
Was heaven to her eyes.
Morning time her path to work
Was ever through the park.
Returning home this much loved way
In sun or nearing dark.

Like Eden, evil was around
To ruthlessly deface
Love, beauty and all innocence
Within this favoured place.
For she was found, defiled and dead
In the morrow's chill alarms,
On grassy mound among her trees,
Beneath their mourning arms.

A Cotter

THREE WISHES

I dreamt one day of an elf.
As he sat upon my shelf.
I asked him, 'Who are you?'
And he replied, 'My name is Hugh.'

'Tis three wishes I give,
To those who see me.
Be positive -
Ask and we shall see.'

First I asked for laughter
And with a smile he gave,
A banana skin for afters,
If I would but behave.

To my second wish
I gave much thought,
A man, and dishy,
Is what I sought.

To my disdain,
He caught me again
A dinner set
Is all I get.

Just one wish left,
My life is bereft.
A good deed
Is what I need.

I slipped upon the banana
And thought 'Oh what a nana.'
To my aid a young man came
And with laughter he took me hame.

Tricia

MRS NOAH'S JUMBLE SALE

Mrs Noah, bored with floating round
Preparing swill all day,
Decided that the animals
Should start to pay their way.

So she took out things she'd salvaged
When the rain began to fall,
Pulled out a large table
And set up a jumble stall.

The cheetah who was first in line
Bought a spotted coat,
The rhino got a nice white horn
And two more for the goat.

The hippo, sick of getting stuck
When going through the door,
Invested all his money
In a sharp and shiny saw.

The caterpillar bought a leaf
The elephant a trunk,
The bold hyena, just for laughs,
Some perfume for the skunk.

And the snail found a bargain
While searching through the stack,
A grey and hardened shell
That's now the house upon his back.

Joyce Walker

A Consequential Tale

The tortoise and hare,
Thought they would share,
A nice big cream cake for their tea,
So they went to the shop,
At a crawl and a hop,
And looked in the window to see,
A chocolate èclair,
'That looks nice' said the hare,
But the tortoise said 'That looks too sickly,
I'm really not sure,
'cos I've had one before.'
The hare said, 'Oh do hurry, quickly!'
A decision was made,
The money was paid,
A big strawberry tart, topped with cream,
The hare grabbed the tart,
Then ran off, 'Where's my part?'
Said the tortoise, so slow, in a dream.
The hare arrived home,
Ate the tart, all alone,
The strawberries, the cream, every crumb,
The tortoise, now late,
Found the tart had been ate,
And said to the hare, 'I want some!'
The hare felt quite ill,
Had turned green at the gills,
With pain in his strawberry-filled tummy,
The tortoise, then said,
As he pulled in his head,
'I'm finding the consequence funny.'

Jim Sargant

Carmody's Vision

A misty view in lenses blue and mask obscured face
The cylinder ticked life's air in time, slowly in no haste,
The tattered paisley armchair had long seen better days
The window danced with sunlight that set into his eyes.
Suddenly with vision anew, he watched his grandkin play
His daughter and son embraced him, a visit from away.
His wife much younger with beauty and smiles
Waltzed gaily to their favourite song
He lifted a frail hand to touch her, a ripple, vision gone.
Underground with pick in hand, he touched the golden coal
Adjusting his lamp, behold, his own kindred souls,
They told him tales, tasted tea, cheese and bread
He laughed feeling warm comfort, gone cold bereft.
Outside strong the scents of heather and pine
And a freshwater spring, with a taste of sweet wine,
He took off his boots urgent, to feel cool delight
Relaxing without pain, till morn turned to night,
Till a welcoming voice, softly called out his name.
'Carmody my son, come hither 'tis time, awaits heaven's stairway.'
Smiling free, he climbed.

Jacquie Williams

ODE TO HRT

What can I do with my hormones?
They're really ruining my life.
When I spot my two little angels,
I start screaming like a fishwife.

Tell me how to manage my hormones?
It's like being a teenager again.
I'm starting to fancy the builder,
And he looks like a dog with the mange.

How can I manage my hormones?
With just one drink I start a fresh flush.
Boiled beetroot used as face powder,
Couldn't possibly make me look worse.

I'm sure it must be my hormones,
I think I'm growing a beard,
Where my skin was always like velvet,
I have stubble and look oh so weird.

Dear Doctor please help with my hormones,
I've gone fat and everything's dropped.
Tell me will I be like it forever?
Or when I'm ninety, will it have stopped?

Maureen Davis

OUT OF THE BLUE

I slipped beneath a patchwork sea
of blues, greens and
turquoise hues, to find
a stunning coral garden
beautifully designed.
Shrubs, fans, plates and domes
spread before my eyes.
Fish of every colour roamed
the spangled reef in shoals,
sprang from shadows,
stared as they went by
like winking ghosts.
Then from the far-off haze
out of the blue he sprang;
the shark, prowling his domain.
Serenity dispersed. Fear and panic
rose, gripped my throat,
choking every breath.
Head to head, eye to eye,
I was his prey . . .

A distant bell somewhere tolled.
The telephone.
Dragged from the jaws
of certain death,
put down my book.

A moment lost in time
       left hanging
              in the air.

Jackie Warren

MAISEY

I own three Border Collies, I've worked with Labradors,
But now I fancy something small, a dog with little paws.

So off I go to Hereford, to see a friend of mine,
She says she has some little pups, to see them would be fine.

It's here I first met Li'l Maise, a Terrier cross-bred,
Her coat is smooth, the colour brown, 'I'll have this one' I said.

So in the car back home she came, to join the happy bunch,
With Collies Gemma, Fen and Nell, her new life has begun.

She really settled very well, she grew but stayed quite small,
Trouble is her attitude was though she's eight feet tall!

She strutted round the living room and slept upon the bed,
But Collies knew this little dog was really not a threat.

I trained her in agility, I thought it'd be such fun,
To channel all her energy and see how fast she'd run.

She really did enjoy it and thought it such a game,
But then one day out rabbiting, she suddenly went lame.

I took her to the veterinary, about her 'wobbly' gait,
'She has a dislocating knee, I'll have to operate.'

So operate is what he did and sorted out her knee,
'Now it's up to you' he said, 'to rest her is the key.'

As the days and weeks passed by, her knee it healed well,
And running round she soon was seen with Gemma, Fen and Nell.

Twelve months later here we are, Maisey's looking good,
But still she goes off chasing after rabbits in the wood.

I wouldn't be without her though, she's fun to have around,
And when the winter evening's here, curled on my lap she's found.

Jane Birch

The Return

The old house stood empty the years took their toll,
paint peeling on sills and the door nailed firm closed.
With stories abounding of what caused time to
roll past with no occupation and what had transposed.
Was it a murder? The gossips had fun with tales
of massacres preventing a sale.
Then one morning a visitor stood in the garden
the story now excalating the neighbours turned pale.
The killer returning to the scene of his crime?
Come to gloat over what he had done?
Released from the prison that held him for years.
One visit, three hours and then he was gone
But then there were stirrings within the strong walls.
An earthmover ripped into the garden's neglect,
the doors and the windows torn off, then replaced
decorators turned up with no lack of respect.

Like a Phoenix arising from ashes laid bare,
A mansion arose from the wreck, with columns
uncovered the neighbours just stared open-mouthed
at the now-finished project.
One day he was back, the curtains now hung, opened wide
to let in the bright sun and they stood there, still gaping
as he stared straight back with his eyes all a-twinkle with fun.
A shadow in the shop doorway was cast as he entered to order cigars.
No pale skin to resemble a man kept behind bars.
As he spoke with a local accent an old lady stepped from the crowd.
'Hello John!' she said, 'I was your teacher in your music class.
I always knew you'd make it when you left to be a singer, it's
wonderful to have you back at last.'
But I asked if he were a guest.
My pal replied he was unknown and not recognised by the rest.
So he wasn't at the gathering, just passing in the night
and the hotel was a long way from my home.

I'd love to say we met again but no, it didn't happen,
Still I often wonder about that night when sitting on my own.
The group he was with could have just been his friends.
He could really have been Mr Right, but we parted without a word being exchanged.
The literal ships in the night.

Channon Cornwallis

BENGIE TABBY CAT'S CLOSE SHAVE

Bengie rose excitedly, it was the day of the May Fair
Meeting Cousin Rupert Black Cat, he simply had to be there
Bengie had been curiously watching, for the last hour
All the people climbing the steps of the church tower

At last the coast was clear, the chance he'd waited for
As he crept towards the stairway, pushing ajar the door
He then stealthily climbed the steps, to the very top
Trying hard not to slip, it would be a terrific drop

Once on the tower roof, he could see for miles around
All across the village, towards the nearby town
He wished Rupert was with him, he really missed his pal
Looking down made him feel giddy, he started to miaow

Suddenly the door blew shut behind him, with a loud bang
Realising that he was now stranded, panicking he began
Bengie knew he'd been foolish, wishing he'd stayed away
He feared he'd be stuck up here, for the rest of the day

He decided to take action, jumping to the lower church roof
Seen by many of the crowd 'a cat up there struth!'
Bengie clung to the stone, but his claws could hardly grip
He was terrified he would fall, if he started to slip

The vicar arrived at the scene, to see what was going on
Assuring the Fire Brigade would be here, before very long
Rupert was anxiously pacing, up and down in the church pews
He couldn't bear what was happening, he prayed for good news

Once there the fireman raised his ladder, up against the wall
Then taking Bengie in his arms, so he wouldn't fall
Bengie couldn't stop shaking, though he was on the ground
He just longed to be home, where he'd be safe and sound

The vicar thanked the fireman, for Bengie's life he'd saved
Rupert was trembling, at the thought of his friend's close shave

Linda Brown

My Grandfather

So slow, you scuffed your slippered feet along our village street
Slow enough for me to watch the progress of egg-bearing ants
Sent scurrying when I kicked a stone from where two hedgerows meet
Or for me to pick our rabbits' lunch from tall cow-parsley plants.

An hour it took us to traverse the half a mile from church to home
An hour in which you showered riches upon my tiny, fair-haired head
Filling it with the ancient tales you gathered from the fertile loam,
Weaving a magic story of the countryside with every word you said.

So slow, your love grew in my heart as we walked those carefree days,
Slow as the lone dove you saw like an angel, circling over and above,
While you pumped the old hand-organ when we sang our hymns
                                                                          of praise.
Such a white dove, I see it still, your endless and unhurrying love.

Pamela M Henderson

JUST PASSING BY

Hello, how are you today? Well, I hope.
Just missing you and wishing
we could talk, or see you for a moment.
Perhaps take a little walk. Hello, how are you today.

Are you laughing, or speaking, busy with it all,
- like bees. Did you see the sun shining - on
leaves, in gardens, squeezing between trees.
Just wanted to talk. Hello, how are you today?

Hello, just to see you and be pleasant
With brightness and ease. To ask
Nothing of each other but find so much to please -
in speaking. Hello, how are you?

Picked fruit early in the morn, all damp in the dew
And wished I'd been sharing all of it with you.
Saw bee and butterfly fuss around a flower - wished you could have been there
To share that magic hour.
Heard a bird speak lightly of the sky,
Stopped and listened to its song
And wondered why, I could not make it last, that moment,
Before it passed along.
Hello, how are you today?
Wish I could see your face. Are they telling
you jokes, leaving you some space?
Is it easy, does it flow. Does life touch
you lightly. I do hope so.
Hello, how are you?

Did you run with your little one
holding her hand?
Did she smile and play?
Did you understand?
Have you laughed a lot with her
when she tried to speak to say,
Hello, how are you today?

Well, it would be nice just to see you and say lots of nothing. Be
inconsequential and careless as you draw, paint and sing.
Hello, how are you with the sun upon your hair
Playing on your beard, reflecting eyes so clear.
Oh, how are you today making others feel alright,
Humming your tunes that you will play tonight.

Just want to see you and to say all the
Little things that happened to me today.
So hello, hope you are bright and strong,
Being just yourself, which is in itself a song.

Well, must go now but it's so nice - just to chat
Exchange some golden banter with eyes which
speak so gaily of just this, or them, or that.

So hello and cheerio wherever you may be
It's always such a joy whene'er you speak to me.

Hello, sure, it's been alright today.

W M Francis

TO MY DARLING HUSBAND ON OUR 47TH ANNIVERSARY

What is love? Let me define.
Love is life, yours and mine.
Two people, yet only one.
If you should go then mine is done.
Sharing closely through the years
Laugher, sadness, joy and tears.
Caring for each other more
Than we ever cared before.
Love, you are my constant friend,
Walk beside me till the end.
Then whoever death invites
Waits till paradise unites.
I've loved you dearest from the start.
You are the keeper of my heart.
Keep it safe, forever true,
For I belong to only you.

Heather Feetham

The Owl

Once upon a long time,
A friend bought me an owl,
A replicated ornament,
With claws clutched round a dowel,
The details were so lifelike,
Its colours warm and bright,
I have never seen a real one,
Only heard them hoot at night,
My birthday brought the next one,
It was sculptured out of coal,
The workmanship incredible,
It moved my very soul,
Crystal was my Christmas gift.
Its markings finely etched,
This wondrous bird two inches tall,
Stood there with wings outstretched,
These proud, and beautiful, birds of prey,
For whom I hold great affection,
Made up my mind right there and then,
I would start up a collection,
My next step was a journey,
To the sanctuary, there I went,
I didn't see just two or three,
I beheld a parliament,
There were little owls, and tawny,
Long-eared, amongst the leaves,
Short-eared, and the screech owl,
And barn owls in the eaves,
My wish was finally granted
And to my great delight
At last I'd seen a real one,
Not just hear them hoot at night.

Twaa Bowcock

My Mum

Why are you so special and such a joy,
you love me lots and love my little boy,
why are you so special, a hundred reasons why,
you are good, kind and fun and that is no lie.
In anticipation and delight,
my little boy looks up to you
in everything you say and do,
that's why his granny is so special
and thinks the world of you.
But is there any wonder,
he loves you very much,
like I do, your daughter,
you have given and taught me so much,
you will always have a special place
in our hearts without any doubt
and lots of memories to cherish
and if anyone should upset you
we would certainly shout.

You are my mum and I love you
but you are also my best friend too,
what would have become of me,
if it had not been for you,
no do not be modest,
I owe everything to you,
you have always been there
through thick and thin
and I love you for being you,
and loving us within.

So what I am trying to say,
is do not despair,
I know you miss Dad,
I am very aware,
but you know he sees us all
in everything we do
and I know in my heart of hearts
he is keeping an eye on us,
and especially on you.

Jill K Gilbert

HATED SIMPLY FOR BEING ME

As the sunlight glares through the window of my humble abode
And the leaves on the trees, shiver with the rushing of the breeze
I remember the days back then

We were so young and so in love
No one could separate what we held inside for each other
Try as they might, well they tried with all of their might

Ten long years of walking on egg shells
Tiptoeing around like a frightened lamb
Didn't dare say anything out of line
Didn't dare speak my mind
For fear it would cause an almighty row

I never fitted in, I wasn't good enough
I was taking the little boy away from his mother
He could have done much better than me
These words rang out, in that familiar tone of voice
I was a low-down scumbag, I belonged in the gutter

They never treated me with respect
The respect I was brought up to treat an adult with
They ridiculed me, mercilessly
Passed insults at every opportunity
They were all take and no give

Not anymore, I took a stand
I made them see, they could not suppress me, for being me
I am a person with feelings and intellect
They treated me like I was not worthy
But I showed them, I showed them my inner strength
and they could never make me crumble.

Jane Smith

KANADA

Herded into railway carriages
Barely room to breathe
Few of you would return
To the places from where you leave
Promised relocation by the Führer
A new land, of hope and dreams today
The words so hollow on the sign
Simply, it read Arbeit Macht Frei

Many of you dreamt of a land
Freedom to be who you wanted
Only your possessions got there
A collection of what had been looted
Stripped of your clothes and hair
You walked to the show so innocently
The last twenty minutes of life
It wasn't long until you became free

Pointing out who was fit or not
Killed by the ones who should have been
The only certainty was suffering
They lived the days you could have seen
Separated from your family
Not knowing it was for the last time
How could anyone possibly be so cold?
The young slept without a nursery rhyme

Kenny Morrison

GRANDMA

'Some say it is a woman's right
But, more than that, a basic need.'
My granny laughed when I said this,
A twinkle in her eye.

'We had no choice when I was young.
Enjoy yourself a while: a job,
A flat, a car and money, too -
Girls like you don't know you're born.'

I told myself, 'Perhaps she's right,'
And smoothed her lacquered nails.
I sighed. 'You win - I'll wait
And be a mum at fifty-eight.'

Gill Morgan

PRECIOUS MOMENT

When my fourth grandchild was six
Suddenly, it came to me
That he could be the last one
In our growing family

With just the one granddaughter
This thought, I dwelled upon
That she'd remain outnumbered
By my grandson's, three to one

Though in my early sixties
My maternal instincts rose
I! couldn't have any more
My daughter's might, I supposed

Then a call came from my youngest
Just as though, she'd read my mind
To say that, she'd been trying
For another child some time

After three miscarriages
Our tears, would have filled a well
But determined she never gave up
Only time itself, would tell

For the fourth time she conceived
And this time, successfully
I heaved a sigh of relief,
As each month passed problem-free

At last! that precious moment
When I viewed the many charms
Of Hannah, my new grandchild
For the first time, in my arms!

Patricia Whittle

WARTIME OASIS

'When the war's over we'll marry,'
The engaged couple agreed,
But the brutal First World War dragged wastefully on.

Nineteen eighteen brought real hope,
So the couple fixed their date.

Dolly's father, a cabby,
And a man of limited means,
Enquired at work about transport.
'Take the best,' said his employer.

The day before the wedding,
Ben arrived from Ireland
On four days' army leave.

On the happy July morning,
His parents looked wide-eyed
At what had halted outside:
Not the expected cab,
But a carriage and two dapple greys!

Soon, the delighted bride,
In white, with a red rose bouquet,
Travelled in style with her father
To marry her khaki-clad bridegroom
At their chapel at eight o'clock.

There were no professional photographs
('In case I don't come back,')
Nor even a relative's snap.

But, at appropriate intervals
During the couple's long lives,
Mother would say, with a smile,
'At *our* wedding we had a carriage
And a pair of dapple greys.'

Dora Hawkins

My Aunt And Uncle's House

The bungalow strangely always smelt of kippers!
my aunt speaking in upper class tones
us children sat silently on shiny leather
requesting BBC banality of Jewel and Warris
and leafing through the 'Illustrated' London News
and 'Country Life' which peered out embarrassingly
from under cushions
stalwart in sepia
staring silently from the cupboard
where more relations
defenders of a lost empire and a ruined Raj

Paul Wilkins

HAPPY BIRTHDAY MUM

Eighty years ago in the month of May,
A baby girl was born - this day.
Birds sang out a welcoming chorus.
Blanche - born under the sign of Taurus.

Your family increases year by year,
Three sons, grandchildren, and Leo dear.
Your sons can never do anything wrong
How many times have we heard that song?

We consider you so very lucky.
We're first to admit you're pretty plucky.
You have such lovely daughter-in-laws,
Much better than sons with no flaws.

You're always there to give a hand,
Loved playing with the kids in the sand.
You hold your family very dear
And like nothing more than to have them near.

Organised and independent too,
Bossy, awkward, all these adjectives will do.
We all wish you a very happy day
'Happy birthday Mum' are the words we say.

So eighty years have just flown by,
We're grateful to you and we don't lie.
So thank you Mum for being there.
From your family we all care.

Lin Bisgrove

SAY THANK YOU ... THEN AND THERE
(Dedicated to Abdur Raheem)

Please do not keep saying thank you
for saying at a later date
future time . . . distant occasion . . . I will do it
it may never come again for you
say it then and there . . . at once
that is the suitable time to do it . . . don't

I did not say thank you
orally or in written words to him
I do not know why? . . . still
I am not aware of it . . . even now

Here Father and I used to sleep
in the spacious veranda . . . every night . . . almost
he used to tell me stories
I do not recollect what he narrated to me
or we communicated . . . conversed
except his love, care, affection, feelings
for me within him

He has died and I am repenting
in every moment every day
kaleidoscopic lives, livings
consoling myself to meet him
and then I say . . . thank you . . . thank you . . . very much
when I part from this earthly life
and my soul going to the place where it came from
who knows from where the soul comes from
and where it abodes when it departs

Ghazanfer Eqbal

THE HEIRLOOM

My Aunt Frances passed it on to me.
Shrouded in secrecy she ushered me
Into a private moment, a private past
belonging to both of us but known by neither.

As she tentatively teased it free
of its secret shrine,
carefully clutching the battered brown envelope,
she exposed a black and white
print of a personal history,
hers and mine,
that up till then had never
felt precious to me.

Later that day,
shrouded in secrecy, I tentatively
tucked it into my bottom drawer
knowing,
however alive in others,
it would be forgotten
for a string of time
again.

Now in the present I display the past,
my own and others.
In pride of place,
alongside a vase of vibrant flowers in full bloom,
showing roots pulled away too soon,
paying homage to the union of
two relative strangers that eventually gave me
my heirloom.

Karin-Anne McFadden

DISQUIETED REST

Alone, I respond to
the mind's and body's
need for quiet and rest;
lie back half listening
to music - heedless
of passing time.

Later, it seems not I
who stirs fitfully
but my own Mother
here within me, and
I recall as a child
a sense of trespass
on seeing unbeknown
her sleeping face,
vulnerable, ageless
yet strangely young.
My lips dared scarcely
touch her brow.

I am filled with a
great and gathering
sadness - for her
no longer here
and all mankind,
and rise
        my body
rested, but my mind
distressed.

Louise Rogers

OUR LILLEY

She was dark she was pretty
All men's heads turned to see our Lilley
All delights about the earth
Came to settle on her at birth
The earth was just a flat old place
Before it rounded to her grace, and moulded heaven to her brow
To see the halved flush of her downy face

Her fingertips and little toes
Stayed virgin to the budding rose
And all was quiet about the air
For pretence and chance to linger near

The petals of our Lilley flower
That glisten all around her bower
Smile back to show the wanton ways, the primrose loss
                                        to summer's day

Our heads and hearts are sunk in our hands
To have to share our Lillied love with ragged ribald heaven
And with the sad tinged grey and undeserving dove.

R A Toy

MILLIE

Found by some children
In the middle of the road.
Dropped from a car
By a stranger we were told.

They weren't allowed to keep you
So they knocked on our door.
Asked if we could care for you
One look, they need ask no more.

A fluffy little kitten
With such a pretty face.
We all fell in love with you.
Our home was now your place.

You settled in quite quickly
Joined the kids in every game
And so it was decided
Millie would be your name.

You'd sit upon the mantelpiece
And scratch the wall above.
We couldn't get cross with you
You gave us so much love.

As time passed by the children grew.
One by one they flew the nest.
But you stayed close to us
Your loyalty stood the test.

For eighteen years you shared our lives
To some it may sound silly.
We feel your presence everywhere
We won't forget you Millie.

S A Doughty

THANK YOU FOR BEING MY MOTHER...

Dear Mum
I want to thank you for being my mother
(given the choice I'd have chosen no other).
Thank you for choosing such a wonderful man
to be my father. You made a good choice there.
Now you have reached eighty years old
and I want to say, what I should have told
you lots and lots of times - I love you.

Thank you for the fun we had and the games we played,
for dinners you've cooked and clothes you made,
for sitting and reading to me every night
and being there when I came home from school
and for all our pets. Whiskers, the cat, Joey, the budgie,
the goldfish and even that poodle called Susie!
Thank you Mum. I really love you.

We were happy together, Dad you and me.
I joined the Guides and you both helped me.
Thanks for washing muddy clothes after camp
and cleaning up cooking fires in the back yard.
Thanks for badges sewn on and food packed
for hikes. Later I went to college and you backed
all I did. I do love you.

In fact, you spent all your time caring for me as I was growing
up and then I left home to teach but you carried on showing
me love and now you live just across the road and every day
we can see each other and I am glad to have this chance to say,
in this very special way -
Thank you for being my mum!

Barbara Huntley

UNTITLED

Somebody's son,
He thinks of his dad
As he takes another puff,
He's been a bad boy, bad,
Chucked it all away,
Got hurt too, along the way,
It went deep.
He mixed with others
That were not of his kind.
Got silly, and put behind bars . . . it broke them up
Between father and son,
A precious child he used to be.
Came from a good family
he looks so unhappy the face
Speaks of pain:
His arms bore the scars where the needle meet the vein
I thought when I saw him
And I thought of my son,
Your life could be over,
Before it's begun.

Bessie Thackeray

VERONICA'S POEM

My dearest, sweetheart, Veronica,
You are as sweet as sweet can be.
And I knew right off when I first saw you,
That you are the only girl for me.

When you are in my arms, Veron -
Please don't ever be shy or afraid.
Because I love you so much, it's true,
And that love will never fade.

Yes, in love is what I am
And I know you feel the same too.
I hope and pray that forever and ever
It will always be me and you.

I've drunk too much love
And am well and truly Brahms and Liszt.
If you ever vanished from my sight, sweet girl,
You would truly be missed.

Peter Steele

FAMILY ROOTS

Grandfather was a blacksmith
In the tradition of old
And he lived and died in the valley
Where he was born
Welsh he was, and proud of it
And the Celtic blood that flowed
through his veins like the molten
Metal he often poured.

Each dawn to dusk he toiled
Long hours at the glowing forge
Hammering, shaping the metal
Upon the singing anvil
Many an anchor and chain
Many a shackle he forged
For many a famous ship
Had his stamp and work aboard.

Terry Daley

ELEMENTS OF IDENTITY

You're my total and all I ever need
But if you don't believe me
Then keep this as your receipt
From what I write in a letter
To what I say to your face
Though if your discharm me
I can be as delicate as lace
I know that you know this
Yet it's been a while since we met
I'm sure you'll honour my feelings
As I try to with yours and we're kept
Our love's not a mystery
Though we sometimes are
I'll never completely know you
Even as you are
The way that we live
And things we say
Will continue to get better
As we continue to pray
The way that I see you
And the way you see me
Can always go deeper
If we always learn to be
More keyed in with our souls
More open to each other
Then we'll never cease to grow.

Naomi Elisa Price

CROSSED WIRES
(For John who died young)

He looked out at the evening sun,
a little boy left on his own while
his parents had fun.

His mother spoiled him all the while,
her husband was more strict
he used a dog leash as a strap
this made his son act vile.

Taking it out on insects that he often
burned to death,
the simple acts that parents do later
costs something's breath.

Trails of damage follow others
pay for it through life,
it really is a dangerous job
the casualties are rife.

Jean Paisley

TEA WITH ALEXANDER (AGED SIX)

Tea with Alexander,
Is a magic time to me,
Earl grey or orange pekoe,
His laughing eyes agree,
That nothing could be stranger,
Just lift that cup and see,
For whatever you are drinking,
Becomes your favourite tea,
Or coffee of the finest,
As he lifts his cup to me.
A laughing gleeful liquid,
He tastes and licks his lips,
For toasted fun and cakes of quips,
Makes Alexander's tea.

Mary Hughes

My Dearest Love

I'll see you in Pitlochry,
Where the salmon leap
Where the mist rolls off the mountains
Where the hills are filled with sheep
I'll see you when I watch the stream
Flow steadily along
Till it merges with a mighty roar
Making its own sweet song
I'll see you as the sun shines
Through a watery sky
I'll stand and watch the rainbow
And then I'll wonder why
Two people who had everything
Could throw it all away
Instead of helping each other
Through their 'rainy day'
Their children too have suffered
The pain has left its mark
When realisation has set in
The reality is stark
For now our 'strife' is over
Life's sweet again once more
But alas my 'Dearest Love'
This play has no encore

Janet Robertson Jones

VICKY, BEN AND I

I helped my pregnant best friend Vicky out,
By going to the shops as her scout;
Then I had a strange dream about us,
Going to a hospital with Bella by bus.
Two days later, after I told Vicky's brother,
Me rushing Vicky to a hospital wasn't another;
Urgently and unexpectedly her body's waters had broke,
She had to stay in ,wearing a cloak.
A few days late, her son was born,
He was five weeks premature on the morn';
I drove them both to many Yorkshire places,
And went for Vicky on errands into races.
My travelling was by bus, foot and car,
During Ben's first months I was a star;
I was Vicky's companion during her lonely nights,
Feeding him every three hours gave her frights.
I helped her with some of her duties,
But only she bought him his little booties;
I became a godparent at Ben's Abbey christening,
And I became bored with Fiona Gordon's listening.
I finished my ten year relationship with Fiona,
And showed an interest in Vicky the loner;
I was one of her close male friends,
Another is Ben's father of messages he sends.
Vicky and Ben moved from Sherburn to Wakefield,
Then to a house in Moortown which appealed;
I became unemployed by date June two thousand,
I looked for new employment near Vicky's land.

Ian K A Ferguson

MY PEACEFUL MEMORIES

My favourite place is Letham Glen
Even as a little girl I can recall is when
There were go-as-you please competitions
With acts giving great deal of choice
I even remember the compere
Had a deep croaky voice
Many happy times spent on the putting green
Then we'd go to pets' corner.
It just had to be seen

There were all kinds of birds, monkeys and rabbits too
It was a wonderful place - plenty to do
Walk through the gardens, gorgeous flowers galore
Over the bridges to see what more was in store
Rhododendron bushes, lovely roses as well.
Flowers of fantastic colours with a wonderful smell
Sit on the bench seat and have a wee think.
Sun steamed through the trees and sometimes it'd blink
Or maybe just talk and just reminisce
With all the beauty. Ah! wasn't it bliss
It's no wonder I like the Glen
Its joys never cease.
My own special place
With its own inner peace.

Irene Low

FREE INDEED

We shall call one another by name
at times we may forget,
Upon a working day
we are paid for our company,
Then when all is spoken
we shall go home,
To clasp that little self
of freedom to the individual,
Satisfaction from what
many things my love,
To where I must again
draw the curtains on this world,
Keeping at bay the grotesque
nightmare that would encamp,
If it were not for your eyes
your noble gift of love,
I might I'm sure conform
to this world popular,
Death and taxes are sure
but our love shall endure,
So take my hand to drink
from the challis good,
For I am a simple man
to be embraced by you,
Where is physics or science
in your beautiful embrace,
Who can define such intimate
time no clock or judge,
Oh breath my life

my love so strong,
When I am weak
you pull me through,
beyond the barbaric brew
of harvest time,
That factory place
in me some yeast not bread,
Were I hungry what then
that care like you embrace,
My broken husk
Stained on a concrete bed,
Would your fashion stop
for that grotesque,
Beyond the lights neon
for I have loved,
Today in rags I stand
at your public house,
But you say
you do not know me,
I tell you the truth
you are paid for your company,
I am happy inside
for the sun shall warm me,
My word is not brought
now I am free.

Jeremy Jones

BACK THE STRAND
(For John B Keane at 70)

Back the strand I have walked
between the remnants of bagged up pups
Bright blossoms of anemone
and washed back sheep's gut

A leveret has sprung
from where my foot would tread
Hesitant past a saint tombed isle
Archipelago of the dead

Distant bells have voiced their call
consecrating the wind torn hills
Over cloud chased Coomanaspig
curlews answered shrill

This path rising to a jagged grin
where moon and earth meet sun and sky
In the long grass there to listen
amongst shell and sea song I will lie

Brendan O'Neill

ITS POWER

Come rain or shine
we climb,
we stride forward
our name makes it plain
we mean business.

Our shiny outfit
outsmarts everyone
we are a legend
we are strong
we have the best driver
in the world (undisputed)
we are *Ferrari*.

Kulsum Shaikh

REVERIE

These days -
no one swings the swing.
Still -
but for a breeze's breath
which stirs the seat -
where they sat.

These days,
voices which once rang -
silent -
their spirit suspended.
Held in the clasp -
of those days.

The trees,
where once they climbed,
droop -
Abundant branches weep.
Sad in the silence -
of these days.

Breanach

A Nightingale Kept In A Cage

Nightingale sing now for me
And I swear I'll set you free
Let you out those golden bars
So that you can fly away
And sing with your dear friends
If you would only sing for me
I swear I'll give my love to you
And that I'll set you free

Oh I had a nightingale
Inside a golden jail
And she sang her song to me
A song full of love
That caressed my very heart
And I set that fine bird free
She sits outside my window
And sings songs of love for me

Rodger Moir

GROWING OLD

How you change when you grow old
In fact, it's quite dramatic
You get all kind of ailments
Like arthritis and rheumatics
You change in lots and lots of ways
Time very quickly comes
When your hair falls out
From on your head
And you've got no teeth in your gums
Take no notice of me
Ain't I a prophet of doom
But your skin that used to be silky and soft
Is shrivelled up like a prune
Your feet are all hard skin and corns
And your bones have gone all brittle
In fact to put it frankly
You're in a fine bloody pickle
I can honestly say this though
I have this satisfaction
I may be a bit frayed at the edges
But I still like to get in on the action
Nobody fancies you when you're growing old
They want the dolly birds in mini skirts
Showing their legs so bold
Still I shouldn't say this about the young
Suppose I was the same
I only write in fun
But I love the poetry game

E Budd

Unknown Wealth

You said you wanted humility -
But this was not true. And left me
For him instead - because he gave
Much more to you. Now a sea tide
Crashes in my head. And I
Can make no sense of anything
You said.
You did not want money - but it's
Very funny, how he seems to
Have much. Houses and cars and
Lands, horses and such. No there's
No fear of you ever going Dutch.
Often he buys you a diamond
Or mink - when all I can do
Is sit here and think. Of
Those days far off beyond my door,
You insisted, you wanted, only -
To be poor.

David Hazlett

The Unemployed

If unemployed people are to seek jobs
  then help us by all means to earn a few bob
But pay us a rate that will make us smile
  just enough to live on, or we'll run a mile.

Three-sixty an hour, come on it's a joke
  we are not school kids, but married blokes
With families that we have to feed
  rise it to five pounds, then we might take heed.

Otherwise we are better off, signing for Dole
  and believe me or not, we will not dig a hole
for ourselves, or families, for the sake of a job
  to just be better off by a couple of bob.

And what to we get for our hard graft and sweat
  at the end of the week, in our pay packet
after paying our bills, rent and our food
  not enough left for a pint, we're no fools.

If you want us to work, then give us some hope
  we won't work for nothing, so don't take us for dopes
give us a wage, that's worth working for
  we want to be better off, not remain poor.

Don't give us what you won't work for yourself
  we'd all love to own a small money belt
we need decent wages, sit up and realise
  we won't work for nothing, so don't criticise.

Janet Elaine Hill

MY GREAT GRANDMA

My great grandma
is called Mae
her hair is curly
and so swirly,
she can't walk
but she can talk
so, that's okay.

Lauren Beevers

WHO ARE YOU?

The fire roars with vicious flames
deep inside below the skin
people are vicious mention no names
and you never seem to win
what do you do when your soul is in pain
and your fire burns hard inside?
at least it still burns that's the main
your feelings are easy to hide
does your head spin all day long
thinking of things on your mind?
everything's bad and all's going wrong
no way that you can unwind
the best thing to do is ease all your stress
take it easy be your own boss
forget your worries and that life's a mess
lay on the couch have a beer and doss
it sickens the brain it hurts your soul
why worry chill out calm down
so what you're skint in a black hole
give a laugh a smile don't frown
you're a precious stone that shines through
you're a legend a gem a star
so hear what I say you know what to do
find yourself and be who you are

A Buttress

ODE TO EGO

Keep your feet on the ground brother,
Keep your feet on the ground,
The thing that you search for
Can simply be found.
Don't think about halos,
They don't have them your size;
For if they're too big
They slip over your eyes.
Yet on the other hand, brother,
They may be too tight,
And the pressure they cause
Can give you a fright.
Lift yourself from self-pity,
Put vain regrets on the shelf,
The greatest to have is the knowledge
Of your own misguided, misinformed -
- misunderstood *self*.

Hazel Tealby

IMAGINATION

I play in the garden,
Where I can be
A sailor on the deep blue sea,
A fireman saving lots of lives,
Or King Henry VIII
With his six wives.
I can play for hours and hours
Amongst the trees and pretty flowers,
Until my mother calls to me.
'Come in now, it's time for tea.'

I do my homework, so *they* think,
While mother's washing at the sink.
Dad is busy reading papers,
I get on with my own capers.
In my strange world, there I'll be
Fighting against the enemy,
Being the 'hero' with the name of 'Fred',
Until Mum shouts out,
'It's time for bed!'

I go to sleep, and in my dreams
I suddenly hear lots of screams.
I become the 'hero' once again,
Even though I'm only ten!
I go into battle to save the people
From a monster called the Takputeople
Who is an ugly alien
From the planet Zoonamen.
Yes! I am the 'hero' of the night,
And he runs away in a dreadful fright.

Jacqueline Jeffs

Sunlight

Seeing the low sun cast its shade
The long black shadows that it's made in bars
and pointed silhouettes. A stand of poplars
wearing coronets of papery leaves
still clinging on, regardless of the winter gales.

The smoke black hedges draw a sooty line
round every field, things covered once are
now revealed, no canopy of green to
hide the rooks' nests in the forks of trees,
The lack of leaves means stillness in the winter breeze.

The clear November light painting
a picture of the rosy gables and the chimney stacks,
like new the dullness peeled away
as though they'd been built yesterday.
Not light for light's sake but for how it lifts
the heart and gets right to the part that says
'It's such a lovely day.'

The way the laurel leaves are mirrored
by the sun's bright ray. And later, when it's setting,
and the night clouds coming in edged
black on violet in a golden glow behind
the poplars crowned like seven kings.
Shows everyone - there are some very lovely things.

Sheila Cheetham

Dusty

Dusty's on the telephone
'Dusty? Dusty who?'
Dusty Springfield's on the phone
And she wants to talk
To you.
'Hello, this is Dusty
We have a mutual friend
And we've been talking about
Your brilliant songs
And the poetry you penned
And so I wondered if you'd write me
A song that I could sing
To tell the world
I'm happy now
In spite of everything.'
Dusty's on the telephone
It's not a joke, it's true
Dusty Springfield's on the phone
And she wants to talk
To you.

Rod Trott

A Magic Wand

If I had a wand with fine magic its very essence
I would wave it at the warring leaders of Northern Ireland
So the wand would unsoak their sometimes hate-filled minds
And oneness would be their goal

If I had a wand whose magic could reach so far
I would wave it southerly, that it may travel all the way to
Fear-dimmed Zimbabwe and their leader who does not stem the attacks
On all whites in his, their country:
Racism is not an option my wand would simply say
And the man would immediately call off his tormenting gangs

If I had a magic wand it would then veer easterly
To the dust-covered children of Ethiopia and over the heads
Of their military, who would use all their tactical skills to
Convey every truckload of rice and grain to the most needy, daily
And, when weary, be helped by hosts of Eritrean soldiers

If I had a magic wand, it would not be one but two
One crossing the other and a man hanging, helpless there . . .
Do not ever let me forget the magic through which he erases all hatred
Bitterness and overpowering loneliness
If his followers carry this wand in their hands and hearts
Wondrous deeds will be done.

A McMaster

THE MINUS AND THE PLUS

In everything in life there's a minus and a plus
For every one of them out there, there's also one of us
    I'll let you ponder that one thro'
    To try and work it out
    I see you nodding 'That is true'
    But then again there's doubt
Now to some a mobile phone is a very useful thing
But to others it's a curse with its constant ting-a-ling
For if you ever needed help it would be by your side
But then you realise that there's nowhere you can hide
    The boss can reach you anywhere
    You can't escape the wife
    You start to panic 'What's out there?'
    There's something controlling my life!
Now the internet is another thing, it gives us chance to shop
From the comfort of our armchair we won't shop until we drop
    But don't we miss the little things
    The things that really matter
    When we meet friends, the joy it brings
    When we stop for a natter
Have you worked it out yet, the minus and the plus
For every one of them out there, there really is one of us.

Joan Harland

I'M GOING TO BECOME A POET ONE DAY

I'm going to become a poet one day
The most famous around.
I'm going to become rich one day
Forever making a sound.
Show off my new look
Go to the most posh restaurants in town.
Always standing up
Never looking down.
Money, looks, money, cash, fame, money,
I'll have it all,
Signing autographs,
Taking photographs,
With my most rehearsed smile,
Look into the camera
And crack it!
(With my beauty of course)
No, but seriously,
I'm making a promise to you,
I'm going to become a poet one day
The most famous around.

Rizwana Yunis (14)

SCHOOL HOLS AGAIN!

The final day of term has come
It's not so good for poor old Mum

School hols are with us once again
The kids will drive us all insane

We pray for sunshine every day
So they can all go out and play

'Cos if it rains they won't go out
We really must try not to shout!

We give them books and pens to write
They don't want those, they'd rather fight

We'll play a game - that seems quite fair
Until the board's tossed through the air

Shall we bake a cake? We ask
This could be a messy task

Our houses look like World War III
We'd love to sit and drink our tea

A trip to the shops is a nightmare too
When they all want to go with you

They're not that bad, it must be said
They're really sweet when they're in bed

Six weeks' not long - let's just keep cool
They'll soon be back at lovely school.

Janet Daniels

Victoria Falls

From afar one hears the impetuous,
flowing torrents of Victoria Falls.
A rainforest, thick, verdant, green, guards
this majestic wonder of a disappearing world

Cascading spray, spits with silver droplets
into a full coloured rainbow
and harmonises with the dazzling African sun.

Now in full view, a thunderous noise
emits from the bowels of a shaking earth

Fast gathering turbulent waters, monsoon swollen,
mingle in a giant hullabaloo and pours
over rocky outcrops with gathering speed

With controlled fury she descends into a smoking,
yawning chasm and is now becalmed and restful.
Now released from her travelling turmoil,
she meanders in peace and onward the Zambesi flows.

Alex Branthwaite

BUT A DREAM

Once in a dream,
A solitary
Figure,
Stands alone,
Proud it stands,
Yet ever without life,
Its life seeps away to the proud.

Once proud and tall,
Now poor and old,
The known reject it,
For it is but a fool,
Yet the unknown is concealed,
Beneath its cloak.

It lacks all thought,
For it is merely a dream,
Who will not believe the dream?
For who truly believes they are alone?

Angus Crawford

THE DOME

T he zones are great.
H ow enjoyable.
E veryone had great fun.

D on't miss it.
O ne amazing trip.
M any people are inside.
E xperience of a lifetime.

Shauneen Maria Mitchell (11)

PRINCESS

Princess they call her,
She is only five,
As pretty as a picture
And very much alive.

She came to Buddy's café
With Grandad, whose attention she held.
While we drank coffee,
She sat as good as gold.

Her innocence is beautiful
As is her young face
She sat and charmed us all
With her childish grace.

As she ate off her plate
Inexpert with small fork and knife
I wondered what would be her fate
Happiness and protection from any strife?

Jack Purdom

The Library

Assortment of books, ancient and modern,
Topics of all description.
Such a selection is viewed with delight,
To the avid reader, a wonderful sight.

Searching through pages of historic events.
The professor absorbed in discoveries.
With knowledge acquired - his skills to convey
His findings - to students - with clarity.

Beautiful books, Morocco-bound.
Ancient rites in manuscript found.
Transcribed from Hebrew in foreign lands,
Researched and copied by expert hands.

Books of refinement in poem and prose.
Relating subjects concisely.
Illustrated copies in classic design
Favourite poems preserved for all time.

A quiet room in which to read.
And travel the world in reverie.
Studying theatre, drama and stage,
With just the murmur of a turning page.

Joy M Jordan

BETRAYAL

So white, so innocent,
Curling and soft, with lovely fringéd eyes
Breaking my heart:
Here is the little calf, defenceless, sweet,
Who greets me with his gentle breath,
Who like a flower
Cut off, tomorrow dies.

He knows it not, but strange and lonely, cries
For Mother, warmth and food,
But all are gone.
O God, give comfort,
And stay his fear along the desolate road
To sacrifice.

He must be sacrificed for such as I, and I
The Devil's work have done, and all my days
With harsh deliberate sin torn and laid bare:
O little one,
Breaking my heart, I go
Forth to my prospering,
And leave you there.

Veronica Daniel

For Her Money

Said a girl named Daisy Red
'Can you prove dear artful Fred
You're not marrying me
For my money?' said she
'I'll accept your money now!' he said.

Joan Wylde

BIRDSONG

I love to hear the blackbird sing
When all is quiet, at close of day
The mellow notes console my heart
And soothe much more than I can say.

At break of day he sings again
To welcome in the new spring morn
A cheerful sound in sun or rain
A lovely start to rosy dawn.

As day begins, at four or five,
And morning chases night away,
The birds begin to come alive,
And sing their song to greet the day.

Diana Price

ELECTRICAL HEAVEN

It sits, looking so sad and worn,
Not wishing
To leave its home of;
Eighteen years.

It looks clean and new
On the outside.
Of which, I'm sure
It's very proud.

but on the inside
It's kaput.
It's done its job
And well I may add.

It also knows,
With pleasure and pride
That,
It's going off to retirement
In Electrical Heaven.

Where many a washing machine
And other electrical equipment
Sit in contentment,
Knowing that they've done their job.
So,
Here's to Electrical Heaven.

Lesley-Ann Curdy

RENEWAL AT NINE O'CLOCK

A wind which swept through charcoal-leaden skies
dispelling doubt, mystifying minds
in some obscure upper room - Galilee
that rushing, roaring, gushing gale-force wind
blew away all cobwebs of confusion
swept aside scepticism; filled an aching void
of questions with answers at hurricane-force 12
blowing ignorance to knowledge
in the leaping glow of fierce flames of fire descending
the glow of love revived.

A flame had been extinguished on that gruesome day
faith turned to dead ashes
until Mary breathlessly cried:
'Hey! I've seen Him - alive in the garden'
but no one believed . . .

Heavy hearts now soared and roared with hope
dispelling doubt, mystifying minds
and nuances of death
For now a wind of change breathed fire
soaking the faithful few Jews
with intoxicating power but too early for wine
at nine a.m. Galilean time . . .
bursting wineskins, fiery flames fell
filling a vacuum of despair
each speech fluent in foreign tongues
preaching to busy business men
who asked the burning question:

'What meaneth this?'

Judy Studd

ONE . . .

One more love left
one more lie to fake
one more bridge to build
one more heart to break
one more tear to cry
one more breath to take . . .

Ria Blackwell

SCHOOL YARD

I stand,
I stare,
At a school yard of old,
With the sound of running feet,
And children,
So bold,

I smile,
As I again can see,
Childish games
Of my friends
And me.

Damian Begley

THE ENCHANTED SPRING

Little did we realise,
As we struggled our way through
the cold and frosty winter;
That skies would be so blue.

As you wander through lush meadows,
Now that spring is here,
Tall grasses create backcloths
That make you want to cheer.

Their feathery-coloured heads
Of muted purples and cool greens,
Are interspersed with all wild flowers,
The likes you've never seen.

The lambs, they seem to frolic
As they never have before,
Like a freeze round a nursery
As in the days of yore.

Shallow streams are humming
And mumbling a tinkling tune,
Whilst birds add their fluted notes,
To the rhapsody of June.

Stroll down narrow pathways
Blossomed trees now are shedding
Their petals, floating down
Like confetti at a wedding.

Yes, that's the sort of feeling
This spring has given us,
Feelings at one with nature,
Of joy . . . and hope . . . and love.

Edna O'Hara

THE ROSE

A blood-red rose, so tall and proud
Its velvety head, looked to the clouds
With scented breath, he did vent his rage
As to why he was locked in a thorny cage.

Dandelions and daisies, ran amok in the fields
He felt trapped by his leafy shield
A king amongst flowers, so regal and proud
Outrageous perfection, standing out in a crowd.

People admired him, just for his looks
Stories about him were written in books
Lovers would single him out for romance
A jewel amongst flora, a diamond enhanced.

He looked all about him, surveying the scene
If he were king, he must act all serene
Show all his subjects, when put to the test
He could outshine them, as England's finest.

Children would play in fields all around
Chains they did make, from daisies they found
With a tear in his eye, our rose it did weep
Standing alone, his emotions so deep . . .

One day he was picked to be star of a show
Surrounded by others, his petals did glow
His body was cut, but at last he felt free
The best of the bunch for eternity . . .

GIG

WILL TO WIN

You have to strive, for what you need,
The will to survive is a definite must.
You need effort and trust if you're to succeed,
So listen, take heed, without it you'll bust.
You must determine to see the thing through,
Dispense with the vermin, it's all up to you.
Half-hearted, you'll fail, don't lose sight of your aim.
Your strength is your fame, as forward you sail.

For what you need, you have to strive,
It's a definite must, the will to survive.
If you're to succeed, you need effort and trust,
Without it you'll bust, so listen, take heed.
To see the thing through, you must determine.
It's all up to you, dispense with the vermin.
Don't lose sight of your aim, half-hearted, you'll fail.
As forward you sail, your strength is your fame

Peter J Sutton

Paean To The Generations

Gently nod to sleep the last November roses,
The drooping marionettes amidst the fall;
No longer sunward turn their faces,
But earthward their idle heads turn,
        To contemplate their imminent death.

Frosts chill their last earthly days,
Until carried off on the dragon's breath mist
Subdued; bird spirit land aways
Will too accept the fragrant heart, hip
        That had laughed all summer long.

The flimsy redbreast flits the thorns
With russet cape through rusted shafts,
Throats the airs that shall grace his unborn
When his realm shall tilt towards that loving blaze;
        His children, hungry, in these roses' children.

Seán Rooney

Dementia

I miss her: her approval was so hard to find.
And yet - has she grown deaf or blind?
Does she not walk with condescending air,
Head high, as always? But she is not there.

Before, our strivings could not make her proud.
Age-mellowed now but neither weak nor bowed
Her fangs are drawn but still she rules by guilt -
Her power on our endless imperfections built.

Each day she side-slips more amid her mist
No longer the intolerant perfectionist.
Her anger fades - so do we celebrate?
Alas, our freedom now is desolate.

Outgrown at last, her bitterness and scorn,
Her autocratic march now seems forlorn.
Her eyes are innocent and blankly mild,
Bewildered, she reverts to nervous child.

'Though once she was a ruthless martinet
Her sting has gone, her degradation set.
All her extreme fastidiousness has fled:
God take her soon - she is already walking dead.

A J French

POETIC POSERS

If you have two cars in front of a car and two cars at the back of a car,
How many cars have you got?
Your answer should be three cars, *in which you have not.*
(A digit delusion).

If you count down on your fingers, ten down to five, How many
fingers haven't gone?
I have five which is right, but you have four, which is wrong.
(A traffic light teaser).

I said to my son, 'So you think that you can spell do you?
Then spell the word 'shop' So he said 'S h o p - shop.'
I then said 'What do you do when you come to a green traffic light?
I normally go, but I bet you stop.'

John P Evans

Goodbye

When we started this school,
It all seemed so bad,
Now we are leaving,
We all feel sad.

We've made loads of friends,
Had five years of hell,
But now we are leaving,
With stories to tell.

Leaving the school
To go on with our lives,
The girls will get husbands
And the boys, (maybe) wives!

Five years gone fast,
No word of a lie,
When we leave in June,
We'll all say 'Goodbye.'

When we walk out the gates,
We'll let off a cheer,
The teachers will smile
As we all find career.

This is bound to be
A sad day for all,
The tears will be rolling,
Goodbye, George Ward School.

Jessica Graham

Gossip Is Life

Why do we have to gossip so much!
For some it is the only meaningful crutch.
We need information to keep us fat,
Curiosity only killed the poor old cat.

We turn on our radios to hear the latest news.
It's one of many channels to help us exchange views.
The programmes on TV update old databases,
Make sure we know who's winning the latest races.

We gossip endlessly at work every day.
We need to know all about our new boss's pay,
Whom he likes and intensely dislikes,
So we may measure up and cast the winning dice.

The lunch break is a cosmos of ugly gossip told.
Who did what? Right or wrong? Was indeed so bold!
Reputations are ravaged on the flip of a coin.
Many absentees wouldn't care to be rejoined.

Then off we depart to our extensively-wired homes
To make verbal assassinations on our telephones.
We speak for hours on end, blackening the latest trend.
The added intensity intrigues all; don't pretend!

A world without gossip would be extremely small,
We'd possess toy cannons that fired only soft cotton balls.
Why should we hold on, failing to extract fresh delights?
If nothing interesting ever unfolded to liven up our nights!

T Burke

A Life

I scarcely remember the forties,
The decade in which I was born;
'A game of two halves' or so you might say,
Of war and the ending of war.

The fifties shine brightly by contrast,
I often reflect on those days;
The world we were told was our oyster -
All due to the new welfare state.

And then as the sixties were 'swinging'
(a cultural apex no less)
We most of us married, had children;
In that order I have to confess.

But what springs to mind of the seventies?
Those long years of stress and of strain,
On England, on me, on so many -
Just pain; then an easing of pain.

In theory the eighties were better;
In practice they sometimes were worse,
Relationships, seldom easy,
Fragmenting to cries of 'Me first!'

And yet we've survived through the nineties,
John Major, New Labour and more -
The children grown-up, my husband retired
And me, a mother-in-law.

Enough, let's look forwards not backwards;
What's gone should be left on the shelf.
The future has good things to offer:
The past can take care of itself.

Sheila Burnett

DOUBTING THOMAS

I must confess I'm an atheist,
And I would it were not so,
I'm envious of believers,
And wish I could be too.

If I could be a child again
Believing God was love
With angels hovering over me
Ever watchful for my good

Then I would no longer doubt,
For I believed in what was told
There was a Heavenly Father
Who had a heart of gold.

He always walked beside me
Like a shepherd tending sheep
No one ever went hungry
As we sowed so did we reap.

But today there are children dying
Crying out for food
Their homes and fields all devastated
By either drought or flood

Not man-made disasters
With only ourselves to blame
But coming from the Heavens
Bringing suffering and pain

Where is the loving Father
To whom we daily pray
Why does he allow his people
To suffer and die this way?

Is it because he doesn't exist
In his home in outer space
Could it be the reason why
We have never seen his face?

Winifred Lund

DALEK COUNTRY

The Tardis landed.
With its unusual sound.
The doctor poked his head out
And had a look around.
But his sidekick could not be found.
So the doctor decided to proceed homeward bound.

When he saw a woman eating his dog K9,
'Stop that!' said the doctor,
'He has to travel back in time.'
'Exterminate!' screamed a dalek.
'Terminate!' replied the doctor.
To his gun in his shoe,
Which was something nobody knew,
Splitting the dalek in two.

And this was his cue,
To board the Tardis
With K9 bringing up the rear view.
Then vanished into the blue.

Ali Sebastian

AGE OF DESTRUCTION

The world is on fire
With flames of destruction
When the last ember fades
There'll be no resurrection

When the ozone is gone
There'll be no one to care
The warmth of the sun
Will be too much to bare.

The air isn't clean now
We have so much pollution
But it's gone past the point
Of an easy solution.

Our minds are diseased
With a virus called greed.
We take what we want,
Not just what we need.

The world's slowly dying
Through our selfishness
We're killing God's creatures,
Weak and defenceless.

It spins on its axis
And fights for each day
One day it may give up
And blow us away.

Karen Brooke

Impromptu Departure

Happy exchange to the modern way of life
Their home was their abode
Where their friends dined and talked together
Their company was their delight
Many good and sad memories they shared
Memorable times of the families round about
Children playing and dreaming a dream
One day they may react in real life
Reluctantly the people moved away
They departed like the birds taking flight
To occupy and possess ideal homes
A panorama, they had never visualised
To places where green fields, hills surround
Where flowers bloom in the gardens
And children at play
A remarkable difference, a realisation of modernisation
Embarking to rebuild the future anew
New prospects, posterity in view
A complete new life, and venture
Leaving a previous location for a pleasant environment

Sheila Spence

Dead Man Coughing

Up it spilled,
Blood-speckled and frothy,
Phlegm trickling down
An emaciated lip
And slipping onto
The sodden paper
Which lined mug
And p*** pot alike -

A dead man coughing
In the bedroom -
A shared room, with
Water jug and sputum mug
Left standing on the table -
A family room where
I stood, finger in mouth,
Watching death evade me.

Thomas Wyche

MY BURNING LOVE

My loving Dave, why aren't you here,
the love which is burning inside of me is
like the flame of a fire, which is bright as
can be, the colour stands out,
like you, it is warm and dazzling as can be.

The movement of the flame burning is like
your body, which draws me close each moment
the fire glows, it burns hot and bright, like
the loving passion of the night.

The fire reminds me of the times when you
aren't with me,
but in my mind the fire keeps burning bright.

So while I hold those strong relaxing feelings
in my mind,
I hold that loving hot burning passion of you and me.

When the flame goes dim and it loses its colour,
it means I am losing you,
so to keep the fire burning I have to
keep my mind on loving you.

Anne McTavish

Please Don't Go

Please don't go; don't get on that ship.
For me it would seem a lifetime, for you just one more trip.
Don't leave me now; we may not have very long.
I'm fed up playing the part; the one who has to be strong.
Too often in my life, I've let my love slip away.
Too often my heart is on my sleeve; left on display.
They say that absence makes the heart grow fonder, that's a lie.
You just spend more time on your own; more time to cry.
Parting is such sweet sorrow; just one more fable.
Once you have let your love go; no point to lock the stable.
Don't listen to all those clichés, you won't feel any better.
That won't help you in your agonies, while you're waiting
                                            for that letter.
Once you have found each other, that is not a time to part.
That's when you decide to stay together; that's when you
                                            reach the start.
Please don't go; who cares about the time?
Let's stay together forever; please say you'll be mine.

Ken Mills

THE BODYGUARD

Sam had no time for angels until late last Wednesday,
Sitting watching telly, eating pizza from a tray.
The screen then showed a photograph, a face within a frame,
It smiled and looked Sam in the eye and called him by his name.
Sam sat up straight and felt he had to ask him who he was.
'I'm your Guardian Angel and I'm here tonight because
I thought we'd have a chat,' he said, radiating charm,
'You see, I have this special role, saving you from harm.
I stopped you stepping off the kerb in front of that big bus,
And saved your skin inside the pub when you kicked up a fuss.
I made you change your mind about jumping in the sea,
When you forgot the tide was out as far as it could be.'
He paused a while so Sam broke in to have his little say,
'Well thank you very much,' Sam said, 'But why show up today?'

'Actually, contractually, there's something to revoke.
I cannot keep on guarding you while you drink and smoke.
Their ills are viewed as self-inflicted, that's a well-known fact,
Until you give up beer and fags you jeopardise our pact.
Forgo them and I'll do my best to save you from yourself.'
With that the telly screen went blank, up there on the shelf.
Sam thought about the many things his visitor has said,
And made a silent pledge that night, lying in his bed.
'I'll stop my smoking here and now, and cut out drinking too,
It's said they don't do any good and probably that's true.'
Next morning he forgot about the pledge he undertook,
And lit a cigarette and poured a beer, just for luck.
Arriving at the building site, recalling what was said,
He decided to ignore it, then a brick fell on his head.

Frank Jensen

TOP OF THE STAIRS

Climbing the chestnut staircase,
Past pictures portraying genius.
Shining silks and dusty tapestries,
All the way up from the hall.
Enlivening the panelled walls.
Portraits, naked lovers in eternal embrace.
Stain glass show the genius of Morris'.
At the top of the stairs, one can stare,
Through the window across the park.
London Plane, shades its peeling paper like bark.
Refreshed by a spring shower,
Flowing Horse Chestnuts;
Lawns and flower beds surround.
Willows droop around.
Not a sound;
A peaceful place,
Where a genius has lived.
The silent house,
In shadow and in shine,
William Morris' house like time.
Watches the hours away,
Year two thousand,
Of aspirations.
Embedded into its steadfast walls.
A million millennium dreams;
Just as a poet might seem,
To gaze into space and dream.

B G Clarke

Morning Mists

Early morning mists rising,
in this summertime of life.
Mists are not all that surprising,
when we're living by the coast . . .

In summer, mists refresh your soul,
while sipping down hot tea and toast.
Stepping into the morning mists,
causes one to feel rain-kissed.
While moisture gently falls on face,
and every other flower and place.

Carol Olson

Waiting

It's Tuesday morning and I'm here at reception
I'm full of confidence - but that is a deception
My eye needs attention to put it back right
My stomach is rumbling and I'm so full of fright!

Here comes the nurse who I give my name too.
She looks so important - (bet she hasn't a clue)
A doctor arrives to take down my news -
And look at the theatre staff (all in their blues).

An anaesthetist is important, my life in his hands
He takes my observations and explains his demands!
The surgeon is here - he's drinking his tea
My legs they are crossed. I'm dying for a wee.

I'm first on the list, oh God I'm not ready
I stand up reeling - my feet are not steady!
Nurse marches me along to the theatre doors
'Please! Please! Now can I have a little pause?'

The operation's over, I'm back in my chair
Everyone was so friendly, they do really care
I'm off to my home now, having enjoyed my long day
I hope you have *your* eye done, and it will be okay!

Muriel Turner

A Nice Wee Cat

He is a nice wee cat
Is the cat from next door
Except of course
When he is all out for war
It is then that he fights
Like a wild dervish devil
Believe me he does
Yes he does on the level

He is a playful cat
Is the cat from next door
He always sneaks into my house
Then he plays upon my floor
Whirling and prancing
Doing his cat dancing
Snuggles up to my toy cat
Tries on his romancing

But he is a nice wee cat
Is the cat from next door
He comes in for his dinner
Cleans his plate then looks for more
His name is Felix an admirable name
Without all his visits
Life would not be the same

He is a nice wee cat
Is the cat from next door
He takes over my house
Sits on my best chairs not on the floor
I wish he were mine, I bet you do too
The black and white kitten cat
All cuddly almost new.

Eleanor Dunn

REMEMBER HER

The changing scenes Her Majesty has seen
Seem to have helped her through the years,
How many times have we seen her in laughter
Never does she show her tears.
Training we know is given, to all who sit upon the throne.
But this young beauty has surpassed all time.
For many years now she's been alone,
Everyone will remember her in years and years to come.
Our lovely and regal lady, 'Elizabeth' our Queen Mum.

Betty Worley

CAT CAPONE

He stares,
  Distinctly disturbed,
As he nestles uninvited by my window,
  Playing 'Bonnie and Clyde'
With the new kitten.
  He offers her an evil paw,
Inviting her to join The Mob,
  Touched by Siamese or not,
She'll do okay for his next 'Italian Job'

  This is Mr Boss Cat,
With penetrating Mafia eyes,
  He won't even hear her distraught cries,
As he sends in his spies.
  And prepares to do battle,
Ready or not!

Margaret Phillips

REFLECTION

Glimmer of light on sea and shore reflects
highlighting infinities meeting; wrecks
sunk from calamities past without trace
silting machinery glorious - face -
ghosts forgotten held safe in metal nets.

History competes in singing - are flecks
still showing in special pattern of specks
original sin emissions through grace
glimmer of night on sea and shore.

Plain Duckworth oil in engine clears not decks
festering still, with rust rotting all - let's
not shift - carry the load - baggage fills case,
refuse until boat sinks - fish vomits - race
equalises - humans - let up God; whets
glimmer of light.

Robert D Shooter

LONELINESS!

What is 'loneliness'?

Is it the time, when a friend leaves for home,
And once more we're left on our own?
Or is it the time when a loved one has died,
And we're left to face our lives alone?

Time's a great healer and we will find,
That eventually our hearts will mend.
And the telephone's there close to your side,
Whenever you want to call up a friend.

Loneliness to me means so much more,
Like a garden where the birds never sing.
Where the earth is stony, barren and damp,
With no flowers to herald the spring.

That's where the houses look shuttered and barred,
Like your neighbours had all moved away.
The sun doesn't rise in the morning,
And the sky remains cloudy and gray.

It's a garden untouched by our Lord's hand,
Where no man on earth wants to be.
For within its walls we'll find Satan,
And our souls would never be free.

And it's there in that bleak little garden,
So silent we hear not a sound.
The garden I never will enter,
For loneliness is waiting to be found.

M Muirhead

AFTER LIFE

People are ignorant and blind to see.
No one lives for eternity.

We only live once and only get one try.
There's no more life after we die.

Some people believe in heaven and say it is God's nest,
But in heaven only the good can rest.

Others believe in hell with the fear and the pain.
But this is a place for evil and insane.

Surely forever is too much to give.
A lifetime is enough for anyone to live.

But people are ignorant and blind to see
That no one lives for eternity.

Darren Abbott

INTERTRAVELLING

When I wish to do some travelling within the comfort of my home
I can switch on my computer to visit foreign lands
I click onto the Internet to see where I will go
Perhaps I'll go to Africa, Hong Kong or Mexico
Maybe I'll go to Russia, Down Under would be nice
Or travel up the Amazon - such instant world-wide choice
When I've been to countries far and wide
And need no more to roam
I'll point straight back to England
Briefly stopping off in Rome
When my journeys have all ended
I return to seek my house
Someone inside will be curled up there
It's that long-tailed PC mouse.

Miriam Thornicroft

The Authentic Western Night

I bought the buckskin trousers, the cowboy boots and hat.
Then I bought a real expensive six shooter, by mortgaging my flat.
I'll admit I looked a million dollars, as I walked into the place.
I enjoyed the admiring glance, from her rugged, weathered face.
I was challenged to a shoot out, and yet I had no fear.
I had practised day and night, I was good, that was pretty clear.
I cleared my holster first, and shot him in the chest.
I felt a pain in my arm, and blood shot on my vest.
I watched in amazement, as the blood ran down my arm.
I shouted out, 'I have been shot,' to everyone's alarm.
The stranger walked over, gun still in hand, he asked, 'Are you alright?'
He said 'I like things authentic.' and he strode into the night.

Don Goodwin

NEWCASTLE STAFFS CARNIVAL

I went to Newcastle Staffs Carnival on Monday 1/6/2000
and was delighted to see the crowds!

Then stacks of plants and bought a couple
I went round with Nelly - a pal!

I sang and clapped to the drums
and the Fiddlers Three which woke up me!
A familiar beat, a real treat!
Then the Irish tap dancers in red, blue and green
all in rich gold-trimmed velvet so smart on their feet!

We also saw ABBA
in red suits and gold capes
the guitarist in a white suit and gold cape!
The pianist in white shirt and long black hair!

Then the procession: -
of hip-slapping lasses
so bright in numerous colours
and beat-keeping feet!

The floats of picturesque scenes
and no less, a quartet of musicians!

Marie Barker

FROGGER!

There once was a frog called Frogger
Who bounced into action on a log.
He escaped from his pond -
With whom he had no bond,
And found himself captured on a computer game!

The researchers found out what his name was,
So they used it on this brand-new game,
Frogger thought he had made a terrible mistake -
He felt deeply ashamed,
But really, he had just found fame!

The game went like this -
There were nine fantastic three-d worlds,
And each time Frogger lost all five of his babies.
There was so much danger, no time to rest,
On these fun and action-packed quests!

Christine Wayne (12)

SUPERNATURAL

A mirror away from a dimension.
A lonesome silence,
stood alone,
with a room of synthetic objects,
waiting for a natural reaction,
a force from the spirits,
against the creation of a human,
a water so deep,
a wind so strong,
an earth so solid,
a power so moving,
in a fearless circle,
north winds,
and the creation of air and invention,
casted within the heart of the natural,
to seek that power
waiting to be evoked.

Amy Holland

Who Needs Reflexology

But there is nothing wrong with me
What I mean to say is 'nothing you can see'
I just feel lousy and fed up with life
The world is going west and full of strife
Maybe I will try a touch of reflexology
Already after an hour I owe it an apology

The sun is shining and it's very bright
The birds are all singing in sheer delight
My neighbours are smiling and waving hello
But my friends tell me it is always so
It must be me for getting so low
I must now change my line
For me, Reflexology works fine.

Paff

THE SLAB

For twenty years it had lain in place
Its origin unknown without a trace
Unimportant it appeared
Dirty, ravaged by the years.
Yet, what started as a joyless task
Became an eye-opener, surprises unsurpassed!

Beneath its hidden space
A mysterious, alive, frenzied place.
Suddenly exposed to the light of day
Privacy surrendered, taken away.
Worms, some many inches long
Uncurled, unfurled as if to song
One, fat, transparent like a mobile vein
Headed for the nearby drain.

Ants scurried to and fro
A beetle emerged, black, aglow
Insects of every size and shape
Concentrated on a quick escape.
A centipede took off as if jet-propelled
With its many feet speed upheld
Thousands of tiny eggs projected future life
Nature's circle, breeding rife.

A slug held on tightly in its slime
Followed by a translucent line
A ladybird rested on a leaf close by
Adding to the visual joy.

Roots criss-crossed every inch of earth
Tangled, knotted, broad of girth
Pebbles resurfaced as if on cue
Reinstating their place anew.
Beneath this slab lay buried treasure
Nature's gift without measure.

Suddenly it broke in two
Falling awkwardly, all askew!

Gloria Hargreaves

THE CLOSING SUMMER DAY

Oh how glorious the peace of summertime,
The afternoon sunlight tapered by the shade of trees,
The hazy sky a hum with bees,
The morning sun less fiercely glows,
Lowering in the sky, the shadows grow,
Dappled long silken grass,
Deflect the rays of golden cast,
The apple trees burst out with blooms,
With summer flies that flit and flume,
The birds less busy now retire,
To lower branches in pairs inspire,
To sing harmonies octaves higher
And refresh on breeze in sunset's fire.

Joanne Collinson

SUBMISSIONS INVITED
SOMETHING FOR EVERYONE

POETRY NOW 2000 - Any subject, any style, any time.

WOMENSWORDS 2000 - Strictly women, have your say the female way!

STRONGWORDS 2000 - Warning! Age restriction, must be between 16-24, opinionated and have strong views.
(Not for the faint-hearted)

All poems no longer than 30 lines.
Always welcome! No fee!
Cash Prizes to be won!

Mark your envelope (eg *Poetry Now*) *2000*
Send to:
Forward Press Ltd
Remus House, Coltsfoot Drive,
Woodston,
Peterborough, PE2 9JX

OVER £10,000 POETRY PRIZES TO BE WON!

Judging will take place in October 2000